WALFORD DAVIES

Dylan Thomas

NORWICH CITY COLLEGE LIBRARY

Stock No.	94109	
Class	821.91	THO
Cat.	Proc. /	

Open University Press
Milton Keynes · Philadelphia

Open University Press
Open University Educational Enterprises Limited
12 Cofferidge Close
Stony Stratford
Milton Keynes MK11 1BY, England

and
242 Cherry Street
Philadelphia, PA 19106, USA

First Published 1986

Copyright©1986 Walford Davies

All rights reserved. No part of this work may be reproduced
in any form by mimeograph or by any other means, without
permission in writing from the publisher.

British Library Cataloguing in Publication Data

Davies, Walford
   Dylan Thomas. – (Open guides to literature)
   1. Thomas, Dylan – Criticism and interpretation
   I. Title
   821′.912   PR6039.H52Z/

   ISBN 0-335-15092-6
   ISBN 0-335-15083-7 Pbk

Library of Congress Cataloging in Publication Data
Main entry under title:

Davies, Walford, 1940–
   Dylan Thomas.

   (Open guides to literature)
   Bibliography: p.
   1. Thomas, Dylan, 1914–1953 – Criticism and interpretation.
I. Title.   II. Series.
PR6039.H52Z6228   1985   821′.912   86-794

ISBN 0-335-15092-6
ISBN 0-335-15083-7 (pbk.)

Text design by Clarke Williams
Phototypeset by Dobbie Typesetting Service, Plymouth, Devon
Printed in Great Britain by J. W. Arrowsmith Ltd, Bristol

For Brinley and Olive Powell in Wales
and for Hugh Addy in America

Contents

Series Editor's Preface

The intention of this series is to provide short introductory books about major writers, texts, and literary concepts for students of courses in Higher Education which substantially or wholly involve the study of Literature.

The series adopts a pedagogic approach and style similar to that of Open University material for Literature courses. *Open Guides* aim to inculcate the reading 'skills' which many introductory books in the field tend, mistakenly, to assume that the reader already possesses. They are, in this sense, 'teacherly' texts, planned and written in a manner which will develop in the reader the confidence to undertake further independent study of the topic. They are 'open' in two senses. First, they offer a three-way tutorial exchange between the writer of the *Guide*, the text or texts in question, and the reader. They invite readers to join in an exploratory discussion of texts, concentrating on their key aspects and on the main problems which readers, coming to the texts for the first time, are likely to encounter. The flow of a *Guide* 'discourse' is established by putting questions for the reader to follow up in a tentative and searching spirit, guided by the writer's comments, but not dominated by an over-arching and single-mindedly-pursued argument or evaluation, which itself requires to be 'read'.

Guides are also 'open in a second sense. They assume that literary texts are 'plural', that there is no end to interpretation, and that it is for the reader to undertake the pleasurable task of discovering meaning and value in such texts. *Guides* seek to provide, in compact form, such relevant biographical, historical and cultural information as bears upon the reading of the text, and they point the reader to a selection of the best available critical discussions of it. They are not in themselves concerned to propose, or to counter, particular readings of the texts, but rather to put *Guide* readers in a position to do that for themselves. Experienced travellers learn to dispense with guides, and so it should be for readers of this series.

This *Open Guide* to Dylan Thomas is best studied in conjunction with *Collected Poems 1934–1952*, Everyman's Classics paperback, (Dent, 1984). Page references in the *Guide* are to this edition.

Graham Martin

Acknowledgements

The author and publisher are grateful to J. M. Dent and Sons Ltd and the Trustees for the Copyrights of the late Dylan Thomas for permission to quote from his poetry and prose.

The author also wishes to thank Professor Graham Martin, series editor, for wise and patient guidance; and Miss Elaine Stephens for her immaculate typing.

1. Biographical and Introductory

I

'I never thought that localities meant so much, nor the genius of places, nor anything like that'.[1] To some degree, any brief account of the life of a writer has to be an account of places. The thinner the eventfulness of a life, the larger do places loom as contexts for poems and stories. Dylan Thomas's life was at least outwardly eventful enough to have bred a personal legend, sealed finally with a famous kind of death. But in as much as the work draws at all on things outside the poet's own imagination, the real arc of the career draws attention more to places than to events. That arc was from the poet's birth in Swansea on 27 October 1914 to his final settlement in Laugharne from 1949. London in between and America towards the end (and at the very end) called for, and got, performance of the life as well as of the work. But *perfection* of the work depended crucially on other, more obscure, places. Any significance in the fact that those places were in Wales is something we shall leave to later chapters.

However, one thing that has to be noted at the start of even a bare biographical outline is itself something that may have run deeper than the more obvious relevance of 'place'. It is the influence, from the outset, of the poet's father, D. J. Thomas. His first-class English degree and real, if stern, love for literature seem not to have brought the father much personal happiness as Senior English Master at the Swansea Grammar School. But his fondness for reading poetry aloud (especially Shakespeare) met with nothing but eager receptivity in his young son, even if it wasn't an eagerness that was to stretch to any other subject when Thomas finally reached his father's school in 1925. The father's passionate love for poetry was salted by a sense of frustration at not being able to pursue it in ways more congenial to his temperament that schoolmastering. There is some evidence that he had failed to get recognition as a poet in his own right; more certain is that he had considered himself wrongly passed over when appointment to the chair of English at the new University College of Swansea was made in 1920. The disappointment, given high profile by D. J.'s uncompromising personality, may have played a part in the intensity of the son's first experiences of literature and in the early self-consciousness of his determination to be a poet himself. But there was also of course the simpler advantage that the young boy was independently able to take of his father's unusually well-stocked library. And in the same way, any deeper linguistic influences that birth in Swansea may have had do not remove the equally important fact that the town and its surroundings were locations for a convincingly happy childhood.

Thomas attended the Grammar School until 1931. His first poems, and some prose pieces, were published in the school magazine, which he also edited from late 1929. In April 1930, however, he started entering a larger body of poems, in various styles and stages of completion, in some exercise-books, now known as the 'Notebooks'. Four of these, containing poems entered up until April 1934, are extant. His art developed quickly enough for the Notebooks to become the main source for his first three published volumes up until the end of the 1930s. In 1931 he started employment with the *South Wales Evening Post* as a reporter, in which capacity he showed as much regard for the imaginative as for the factual interest of what he wrote. His critical articles in a companion paper (the *Herald of Wales*) on 'The Poets of Swansea'[2] projected more studiedly the image also of the literary young man-about-town. More literal acting talents were exercised through his enthusiastic membership of the Little Theatre amateur group. His circle of friends grew to include men such as the artists Alfred Janes and Mervyn Levy, who had already found a base in London as well as in their native Swansea.

Thomas left the *Evening Post* at the end of 1932. 'And death shall have no dominion', the first poem to gain London publication, appeared in the *New English Weekly* in May 1933; and what was probably his first visit to London took place in August of that year. Poems subsequently sent to Geoffrey Grigson's influential *New Verse* were returned. But a poem sent to the *Sunday Referee* was accepted. It was this paper that also, in 1934, chose him as the second winner in a poetry competition in which the prize was having the paper sponsor the poet's first collection. The first recipient had been Pamela Hansford Johnson, whose now-famous correspondence and friendship with Thomas started at this time. This relationship, and the widening acceptance of his poems by the leading periodicals, including now *New Verse*, drew his ambitions even more decisively towards London. (T. S. Eliot, having seen the poem 'Light breaks where no sun shines' in *The Listener*, wrote to him, showing interest in his poetry; and he was already reviewing books for the *Adelphi*.) Home had become a sadder place since the summer of 1933 when D. J. Thomas had been diagnosed as having cancer of the mouth. The actual move to London occurred in November 1934, and the first volume, *18 Poems*, was published that December. The eighteen had been selected from amongst the most recent poems in the Notebooks. They were poems in which Thomas had newly achieved his most characteristic style, on themes having to do with organic processes. Critical acclaim in the reviews reflected the originality and impact of the achievement.

But Swansea still alternated with London through the middle years of the 1930s. It was in Swansea in 1935 that he first met the poet Vernon Watkins, a bank clerk in the town. The friendship (and their detailed correspondence, exchanging advice and analysis on each other's poems over the next ten years) has a seriousness and sanity that did not have equivalents for Thomas in the literary world of London. There, he got to know most of the leading writers of the day, but also began dangerously to indulge the free-drinking Bohemian side of the legend. Work on new and revised poems for a second volume also made returns to Swansea necessary. *Twenty-Five Poems* appeared in September 1936. Less enthusiastically reviewed than the first volume, it had also drawn on the Notebooks for at least sixteen of the twenty-five poems included.

Thomas met his future wife, Caitlin Macnamara, in London in 1936. At Christmas that year D. J. Thomas, still in uncertain health, retired from schoolteaching and moved to live outside Swansea. Thomas's movements lost such anchorage as they had had in his childhood home. He and Caitlin were married in Cornwall in 1937 and moved to live with Caitlin's mother in Hampshire until the spring of 1938. Money problems were to dictate movements on a family basis from here on. Such small help as was to come from broadcasting had already started. But penury, as well as any deeper appropriateness, was to dictate the couple's settling, in the spring of

1938, in Laugharne. Apart from its own importance to the shaping of future work, Laugharne was only a few miles from Fernhill, the farm on which the Swansea schoolboy had enjoyed his happiest holidays. Thoughts concerning a published collection of his early surrealist short stories came to nothing, but 1938 and 1939 saw the writing of the realistic autobiographical short stories that were published as *Portrait of the Artist as a Young Dog* in 1940. And in August 1939 his third volume of poetry, *The Map of Love*, had included also such early stories as his new publishers, Dent, had considered respectable enough. Material for about half of the sixteen poems in that volume were still mined from the early Notebooks. But Laugharne had also made new poems as well as new prose possible. Amongst these new poems 'A Saint about to Fall' celebrated the imminent birth of his first child, Llewelyn, in January 1939. Henry Treece had already approached Thomas for information for the first critical book on the poet's work[3]; and in December 1939 an American publisher brought out the first selection of his work to appear that side of the Atlantic. Despite what were again slightly disappointed reviews of *The Map of Love*, Thomas had arrived.

But the war had also arrived, and a pattern of wandering from the homes of indulgent friends to that of his parents was re-established. Laugharne had to be left because of debts as well as in search for gainful employment as a writer. He started writing special wartime scripts for the BBC. In terms of new poetry, his output between 1941 and 1944 was restricted to elegies on deaths in the bombing raids. In early 1941 he had seen the destruction of much of his home town ('Our Swansea is dead').[4] The air-raids had also forced his parents to move again, this time to the family cottages at Blaen Cwm, Llangain, again near Fernhill and Laugharne. Returning to Laugharne itself, the young family moved into the novelist Richard Hughes's house in the grounds of the castle. Thomas had decided to sell his Notebooks. Along with an early Prose Notebook, they went to the State University of New York at Buffalo: for the sum of £30! At the same time (early 1941) he started writing *Adventures in the Skin Trade*. This 'novel' continued the fictive autobiography of the *Portrait* stories, extending it to cover the young poet's experiences when he had first arrived in London. Dent rejected it at the time but it was published posthumously in a still unfinished form. Thomas turned again to London in search of employment, and in late 1941 he became a script-writer on the payroll of Strand Films. Between here and the end of the war he worked on some ten documentaries. The work kept Thomas mainly in London, often separated from Caitlin and the children (a daughter, Aeronwy, was born in March 1943), and with means to allow the hard-drinking legend further growth.

But in July 1944 he returned to Wales, hoping to settle again in Laugharne. From his parents' cottage at Llangain, however, he moved instead to New Quay on the Cardiganshire coast. This return to Wales produced the third creative period of concentrated writing, with such poems as 'Poem in October' and 'Fern Hill' heralding the greater accessibility of theme and the pastoral atmosphere that characterize the later phase as a whole. The most famous radio scripts 'Quite Early One Morning' and 'A Child's Christmas in Wales' also came out of this period. And memories of New Quay itself as a place were later to join experiences of Laugharne as the main inspiration for *Under Milk Wood*. And yet it was also the period when Thomas first started sounding out the possibility of going to America.

In September 1945, however, the Thomases returned to England – first to London and then, in spring 1946, to a summer house belonging to the Magdalen College home of the historian A. J. P. Taylor and his wife Margaret, at Oxford. In February 1946 Thomas's fourth volume of poetry, *Deaths and Entrances*, had been published. Critical acclaim for the volume (a print run of 3000 copies was repeated within a month of its publication) finally confirmed his reputation. *Selected Writings* was brought out at the same time by New Directions in America. He also turned to continuous freelance work (scripts and readings) for BBC radio, including work for the newly launched 'Third Programme'. In 'Return Journey' (broadcast June 1947) he dramatized a search for his old Swansea boyhood. A Society of Authors scholarship enabled the family to spend April–August 1947 in Italy, where Thomas finished the poem 'In country sleep'. They returned to a house, secured by Margaret Taylor, at South Leigh outside Oxford. Work on scripts for commercial feature films like *The Doctor and the Devils* and *The Beach of Falesá* (never produced as films, but posthumously published as books) brought him his best earnings to date. This was to add income-tax demands to personal mismanagement at the root of Thomas's subsequent money-problems. But more important at the time was the fact that work on film and broadcast scripts had also ousted the writing of new poems.

This was why Thomas's thoughts turned to hopes of a permanent home in Wales, preferably in Laugharne. They were realized when Margaret Taylor bought for him the now famous Boat House at Laugharne. His parents were already settled in the village, and a second son, Colm, was born there in July 1949 soon after the poet's own move. Thomas returned to poetry at once, writing

'Over Sir John's hill'. But the writing of new poems was still painfully slow, and *Under Milk Wood* was still in effect only an idea. It was also to Laugharne at that time that the first definite invitation came for Thomas to visit America. The idea of American money subsidizing creative existence in Wales looked promising. The first tour (February–June 1950) set the pattern for later ones; it augmented the legend, but eccentric personal behaviour on these tours did not lessen the real success of the poetry-readings in a wide variety of centres, including major university venues. However, very little of the thousands of dollars that he earned came back with him to Laugharne. There, after the first American tour, he made a start on *Under Milk Wood* and returned to poems, amongst them (in 1951) 'Do not go gentle into that good night', addressed to his father now seriously ill, and 'Poem on his birthday'. Accompanied by Caitlin, he left for a second American tour in January 1952. In February his final volume, *In Country Sleep*, collecting the six poems he had written since 1946, was published in New York. This was also the visit in which the first 'Caedmon' record made Thomas's rich reading voice available in that medium.

Back home in May, he worked on the verse 'Prologue' to his *Collected Poems*. The volume was published, to general acclaim, in November 1952. The death of his father a month later deeply saddened Thomas, who was now himself tired and often ill. But he still left for a third American tour in April 1953. It was on this visit that he finished *Under Milk Wood*, for a première reading at the Poetry Centre in New York; and he was offered to collaborate on an opera with Stravinsky. Home again in Laugharne in June, he worked on revisions of *Under Milk Wood* and on the unfinished 'Elegy' on his father's death. He was even more obviously ill when he left for America again in October 1953, and he died in St Vincent's hospital, New York, on 9 November. He was thirty-nine years old.

II

Most of us, before actually reading much of the poetry, will have gained certain impressions about the poet from, for example, his personal reputation, or from a reading of his prose works. The man himself – the Bohemian, free-drinking 'Dylan' – will probably long since have been a familiar figure. More relevantly, his success as the writer of radio-scripts in the 1940s and early 1950s, and particularly as the author of the radio play *Under Milk Wood*, will have underlined his ability to capture the public imagination. This popular appeal, seen also in the comic short stories of his autobiographical *Portrait of the Artist as a Young Dog*, was a considerable part of his achievement at a time when the serious artist appeared to the average reader to be increasingly inaccessible or élitist. And many of the poems, too, may have struck the new reader with this quality of attractive accessibility.

But the reputation may also have had its forbidding side. Exploring beyond much-anthologised poems such as 'Fern Hill', 'The Hunchback in the Park' or 'Poem in October', the new reader may have been warned (before discovering for himself) that Thomas is, elsewhere, a difficult poet. And, as T. S. Eliot once sympathetically put it, 'the ordinary reader, when warned against the obscurity of a poem, is apt to be thrown into a state of consternation very unfavourable to poetic receptivity'.[5] However, one of the main aims of this book is not to act as if the warned-of difficulties were imaginary; it is to proceed, rather, on the conviction that they are approachable and manageable.

Nevertheless, there is important force in Eliot's point about the necessity of being in a state of 'poetic receptivity'. So at the outset I think any poems you have already found, or are likely to find, accessible are a good foundation to build on. Whatever your starting-point, what will most likely attract your interest is Thomas's use of language, his way with words. And it is of advantage to start thinking of this aspect in response to works which readily respond to the question 'What are they about?'. In this way you will be able to consider form in relation to content quite spontaneously. You could well begin by reading, say, the opening pages of *Under Milk Wood*, as an example of where Thomas's style is at its most obviously popular and entertaining. Consider these few sentences:

> Hush, the babies are sleeping, the farmers, the fishers, the tradesmen and pensioners, cobbler, school-teacher, postman and publican, the undertaker, and the fancy woman, drunkard, dress-maker, preacher, policeman, the webfoot cocklewomen and the tidy wives. Young girls lie bedded soft or glide in their dreams, with rings and trousseaux, bridesmaided by glow-worms down the aisles of the organplaying wood. The boys are dreaming wicked or of the bucking ranches of the night and the jolly-rodgered sea. And the anthracite statues of the horses sleep in the fields, and the cows in the byres, and the dogs in the wetnosed yards; and the cats nap in the slant corners or lope sly, streaking and needling, on the one cloud of the roofs.
>
> You can hear the dew falling, and the hushed town breathing. Only *your* eyes are unclosed to see the black and folded town fast, and slow, asleep.

Such prose is obviously resisting the merely functional at every turn. As important as the details themselves is their arrangement into essentially 'musical' movements. Notice how the catalogue of the first sentence is carefully lifted into a different concluding rhythm by the addition of adjectives to its last two nouns. It happens again in 'the horses sleep in the fields, and the cows in the byres, and the dogs in the *wetnosed* yards'. Thomas is clearly listening to his sentences. Verbally, the passage is inventive in quite obvious ways, with the use of transferred adjectives ('webfoot cocklewomen', 'wetnosed yards', 'folded town') or smilingly adventurous adjectives like 'organplaying' or 'jolly-rodgered'. The style is indulgently suggestive. One might even say 'suggestible': there is something alertly opportunist in the way in which something new is squeezed out of a cliché – the town is 'fast, and slow, asleep'.

Under Milk Wood was written in the early 1950s. A little over ten years previously, Thomas was writing the autobiographical stories that comprise *Portrait of the Artist as a Young Dog* (published 1940). In the first of those stories, 'The Peaches', we come across the following description of the parlour at Gorsehill (the Fernhill of the famous poem):

> The best room smelt of moth balls and fur and damp and dead plants and stale, sour air. Two glass cases on wooden coffin-boxes lined the window wall. You looked at the weed-grown vegetable garden through a stuffed fox's legs, over a partridge's head, along the red-paint-stained breast of a stiff wild duck. A case of china and pewter, trinkets, teeth, family brooches, stood beyond the bandy table; there was a large oil lamp on the patchwork table-cloth, a Bible with a clasp, a tall vase with a draped woman about to bathe on it, and a framed photograph of Annie, Uncle Jim, and Gwilym smiling in front of a fern-pot. On the mantelpiece were two clocks, some dogs, brass candlesticks, a shepherdess, a man in a kilt, and a tinted photograph of Annie, with high hair and her breasts coming out. There were chairs around the table and in each corner, straight, curved, stained, padded, all with lace cloths hanging over their backs. A patched white sheet shrouded the harmonium. The fireplace was full of brass tongs, shovels, and pokers. The best room was rarely used. Annie dusted and brushed and polished there once a week, but the carpet still sent up a grey cloud when you trod on it, and dust lay evenly on the seats of the chairs, and balls of cotton and dirt and black stuffing and long black horse hairs were wedged in the cracks of the sofa. I blew on the glass to see the pictures. Gwilym and castles and cattle.

At first sight, the prose here does not seem linguistically as suggestive as that of *Under Milk Wood*. Indeed, what strikes us first is the functional economy with which Thomas crowds in the surprising amount of detail. Yet we cannot be sure that even here certain effects aren't planned and plotted more craftily than we at first suspect. The impression of things gone dead comes across immediately, and has as its central emblems the stuffed fox, partridge, and wild duck in the two glass cases. But it is the human connivance in the ceremonies of halted life that is most subtly hinted. Despite the stuffed fox, 'mothballs' makes the 'fur' that of a fur-coat. China, pewter, trinkets, and family brooches seem neutral enough items – but not when the catalogue is jostled by the sly inclusion of 'teeth'. Or take the photograph of relatives 'smiling in front of a fern-pot': is the fern-pot in the photograph, or (equally suitably) in the room? The very emphasis on photographs (thrice-mentioned) seems appropriate amongst so many emblems of merely represented life. Does the 'tinted' photograph of Annie therefore tie up with the 'red-paint-stained' breast of the stuffed duck? Even syntax may play a part. Thus 'looking through' the fox's legs, 'over' the partridge's head, and 'along' the duck's breast seems to mime the act of taking aim – just as a gun or a camera were aimed to produce the dead emblems enshrined in the 'rarely used' best room. It seems suitable that what is viewed or sighted in this way through the glass cases is the more genuinely neglected 'weed-grown vegetable garden' outside. The stylistic effect of the whole suggests that the author, too, has carefully taken aim.

But some five years earlier again (1934–35), the poet's prose was concerned with very different things. Take this section from 'A Prospect of the Sea', one of the early short stories:[6]

> The boy awoke cautiously into a more curious dream, a summer vision broader than the one black cloud poised in the unbroken centre on a tower shaft of light; he came out of love through a wind full of turning knives and a cave full of flesh-white birds on to a new summit, standing like a stone that faces the stars blowing and stands no ceremony from the sea wind, a hard boy angry on a mound in the middle of a country evening; he put out his chest and said hard words to the world. Out of love he came marching, head on high, through a cave between two doors to a vantage hall room with an iron view over the earth. He walked to the last rail before pitch space; though the earth bowled round quickly, he saw every plough crease and beast's print, man track and water drop, comb, crest, and plume mark, dust and death groove and signature and time-cast shade, from icefield to icefield, sea rims to sea centres, all over the apple-shaped ball under the metal rails beyond the living doors. He saw through the black thumbprint of a man's city to the fossil thumb of a once-lively man of meadows; through the grass and clover fossil of the country print to the whole hand of a forgotten city drowned under Europe; through the handprint to the arm of an empire broken like Venus; through

the arm to the breast, from history to the thigh, through the thigh
in the dark to the first and West print between the dark and the green
Eden; and the garden was undrowned, to this next minute and for
ever, under Asia in the earth that rolled on to its music in the beginning
evening.

We are aware from this that the prose can take us into strange, as
well as familiar, landscapes. In this last quotation it is also clear that
equally strange things can happen to the language, as language.
Consider phrases such as 'iron view', 'time-cast shade', 'the living
doors', 'the first and West print', 'to this next minute', and 'in the
beginning evening'. The logic of each phrase can be deduced from
the passage as a whole – but only if we surrender more fully to an
imagination not our own than was asked of us in the other two prose
quotations we have looked at. You should bear in mind the
strangeness of this last quotation when we come to the early poetry,
with which it is contemporary. In terms of detailed discussion, this
Guide is concerned with the poetry rather than the prose. But at some
stage you should also read the prose works, following the guidance
given in the section on 'Further Reading' at the end of this book.

It will already be apparent that, for this poet, prose is not
something written (to use Milton's phrase) with the left hand.
Thomas himself described the style of *Under Milk Wood* as 'prose
with blood pressure'.[7] Conversely, a man who writes prose in this
way is unlikely to compose stylistically austere poems. And to get
an immediate impression of this fact I would like you now to read
'Fern Hill' and 'The Hunchback in the Park'. I am not going to say
much about them at this stage. We shall come back to them later.
What is important now is that you should experience directly
Thomas's strong, unembarrassed delight in words, his delight in the
music they create and the things they can be made to do. Of course,
the same is true of all good poets; but it will seem more self-
consciously true of Thomas than of most others. The two poems
I've mentioned are sufficiently different to demand each its own kind
of attention. One thing they have in common, though, is something
you may already know Thomas to have been interested in –
childhood, and its recollection from an adult point of view. From
the perspective of the Modernist revolution effected by poets such
as Ezra Pound and T. S. Eliot (revolutionary in terms of subjects
as well as techniques), memories of childhood on a holiday farm or
of a derelict hunchback in a suburban park may strike you as
unadventurous, even curiously old-fashioned, themes. Accordingly,
you might consider what it is about either poem which makes (if
it does) a new or individual claim on your attention. Where do you

find evidence of a conscious delight in language? Do you notice any cases of modified cliché (as in 'fast, and slow, asleep' in the first prose quotation above)? Where would you point to signs of the conscious artist at work in these two poems? And what about his fondness for multiple meanings?

But as I say, as important as answering any specific questions at this stage is that you should experience such poems for yourself before reading any more of this Guide. So please read now 'Fern Hill' (*Collected Poems*, p. 150) and 'The Hunchback in the Park' (p. 104).

2. Poems on Poetry

Let us start this discussion of Dylan Thomas's poetry by taking some poems in which his subject is the character of his own verse. In effect they look back at the earlier phase of his career, 1930–1937. They should, therefore, give us something with which to compare our own response when we come to look at the earlier poetry for ourselves, in Chapter 3, though obviously they are also poems in their own right, not simply documents.

In December 1938 Thomas wrote a short poem, 'Once it was the colour of saying', which evidently registers a turning-point in his career. Here it is:

Once it was the colour of saying
Soaked my table the uglier side of a hill
With a capsized field where a school sat still
And a black and white patch of girls grew playing;
The gentle seaslides of saying I must undo
That all the charmingly drowned arise to cockrow and kill.

When I whistled with mitching boys through a reservoir park
Where at night we stoned the cold and cuckoo
Lovers in the dirt of their leafy beds,
The shade of their trees was a word of many shades
And a lamp of lightning for the poor in the dark;
Now my saying shall be my undoing,
And every stone I wind off like a reel.
(p. 82)
('mitching' = *playing truant*)

On one level, Thomas is quite realistically remembering his early
home in Swansea – on a steep suburban hill, opposite which were
a field, a school, and a park. Also realistic in fact is the more obscure
phrase 'the uglier side of a hill': in his youth the *other* side of that
hill was open farmland. But the poem is also decidedly about
something more internal: the poet's attitude to language and how
it affects his attitude to outside reality. Like Yeats in his poem 'A
Coat' ('there's more enterprise/In walking naked')[1] Thomas
reprimands his earlier poetic style, and promises a change. What do
you think is reprimanded in that earlier style, and what change is
promised? Does this poem make that self-criticism about the poet's
early style reflect also on a question of the subject-matter of the earlier
verse? What do you make of the last line?

DISCUSSION

Interpretation clearly centres on the meaning of the phrase 'the colour
of saying'. The suggestion is that the early style had tended to rely
more on the autonomous properties of words (pure verbal delight
perhaps, with free associations and rhetorical 'colour') than on what
the words actually *denote* in common usage. The implication that
this is essentially a youthful phenomenon brings the following
description of Stephen Dedalus from Joyce's *Portrait* to mind: 'He
drew forth a phrase from his treasure and spoke it softly to himself:—
A day of dappled seaborne clouds. The phrase and the day and the
scene harmonised in a chord. Words. Was it their colours?'[2]
Elsewhere, Thomas himself speaks of 'the colours the words cast
on my eyes' and of the 'shade and size and noise' of words.[3] The
'stone' image in the last line would therefore seem to promise in
Thomas's use of language hereafter harder realism and precision
(disinfecting the 'romance' of language). The aesthetic preoccupation
with words had 'charmingly drowned' the outside realities of people,
places and things, had inadequately embraced them as realistic
subject-matter. As Yeats put it in 'The Circus Animals' Desertion',

'Players and painted stage took all my love,/And not those things that they were emblems of'.[4] This complex inability to think of words just as cool emblems or signs is central to the nature of Thomas's poetry. In this, he responds to language more like a Joyce than a Yeats.

Do you like the poem itself? I personally find it strongly and memorably expressed. I also like the way in which the problem refuses to be simply solved. By that I mean that the poem itself is anything but verbally austere. Consider the multiple meanings that radiate from words such as 'capsized' (appearing *tilted*, in relation to the steep street, but also *the size of a cap*) or 'my undoing' (*my unwinding*, and *the end of me*). Perhaps it promises well, after all, to find such an obvious verbal relish only relatively chastened in the urge towards plain speaking! Other verbal richnesses extend even more widely. For example, I have been able only to hint at the meaning of the final line 'And every stone I wind off like a reel'. Its main image, however, tells us something about the way Thomas still chose to develop his poems, even while talking about the need for change. The image is mainly that of fishing. The stone previously thrown at the scorned lovers in the park has now become either the bait or the weight on the 'reel' with which he plans now to draw them out. The fishing idea points up how consistently water images have been developed from the original word 'soaked' ('capsized', 'seaslides', 'drowned'). But is 'reel' only a fishing-reel? Could it also be a cinema reel – in which case it connects with 'lamp of lightning' two lines back? If so, the yoking of disparate metaphors, as much as the autonomous romance of words, is something to keep an eye on.

A year earlier (1937), Thomas had completed this other short poem, 'The spire cranes':

> The spire cranes. Its statue is an aviary.
> From the stone nest it does not let the feathery
> Carved birds blunt their striking throats on the salt gravel,
> Pierce the spilt sky with diving wing in weed and heel
> An inch in froth. Chimes cheat the prison spire, pelter
> In time like outlaw rains on that priest, water,
> Time for the swimmers' hands, music for silver lock
> And mouth. Both note and plume plunge from the spire's hook.
> Those craning birds are choice for you, songs that jump back
> To the built voice, or fly with winter to the bells,
> But do not travel down dumb wind like prodigals.
> (p. 79)

Surface difficulties can be removed fairly easily. Thus 'spilt sky' is an image for water (looking like the sky because reflecting it). And the phrase 'that priest, water' is probably an echo of Keats's 'waters at their priestlike task/Of pure ablution round earth's human shores'.[5] Another initial difficulty might arise from the syntax. We can see from the second part of the first line that the opening words – 'The spire cranes' – are a singular noun plus verb. But they might first of all have struck us as a plural noun – 'The spire cranes', as some species of bird! It also takes a second look to see the syntax of these lines:

> Pierce the spilt sky with diving wing in weed and heel
> An inch in froth.

The sense is *Pierce the [water] with diving wing [an inch] in weed, and heel an inch in froth*. Though such examples do not remain a difficulty, we shall see later that Thomas's syntax in some other cases is meant to be more consciously ambiguous. But more important here are the central images themselves of 'spire' and 'carved birds'. Reading the poem again, ask what they communicate to you. Consider in particular lines 9–10.

DISCUSSION

Thomas had first attempted this poem in 1931, when he was sixteen, and still at school. We are unlikely, then, to find it *intellectually* formidable. Even when he revised it in 1937, he described it as 'just a curious thought said quickly'.[6] Perhaps we should consider whether it isn't, rather, just a quick thought said curiously. Did you understand, for example, that the 'spire' is an image for the poet? I do think that that is how the poem works. The spire-poet contemplates two different kinds of poems. One kind is imaged as the 'chimes' of bells or as real birds, escaping from the spire-poet and making contact with, or soiling itself in, the real outside world: 'Both note and plume plunge from the spire's hook'. The other type is imaged as the 'carved birds', part of the stonework of the spire, and communicating only backwards to the poet himself: 'songs that jump back to the built voice'. Thomas's fear here is surely a fear of the utter privacy of his verse. It is also a fear (consider that image of carved birds) that his art has become such a careful, technical affair that his poems are in effect carved, lapidary, lifeless. It is ironic to think that Thomas, of all poets, was the one most accused of a careless, free-wheeling lyricism. Consider his response to Stephen Spender's claim that 'Thomas's poetry is turned on like a tap'. Thomas answered: 'My poems *are* formed . . . they are "water-tight compartments". Much of the obscurity is due to rigorous compression; the last thing they do is to flow; they are much rather hewn'.[7] And this claim of laboriously careful craftsmanship is certainly borne out by the evidence of Thomas's manuscripts.

But would 'rigorous compression' adequately account for any difficulty you yourself had in understanding 'The spire cranes'? The difficulty here seems to me to come more from the way in which Thomas tends to express himself completely through images. This forces us to read literally what are in fact metaphors ('spire' for poet, 'stone bird' for poem etc.), because the poem's narrative remains completely inside those metaphors. In this sense 'Once it was the colour of saying' was probably more accessible. There, we were at least given ordinary details that didn't need to be decoded (a writing-table, school-girls, lovers in the park) which in turn enabled us to recognize a metaphor when we saw one. Yet even there, certain of the metaphors seem to take on a life of their own that could very quickly displace, as it were, the actual ideas or things they stand for. Indeed, the idea of the 'charmingly drowned' arising vengefully to 'cockrow and kill' is something to which Thomas elsewhere would be capable of giving much more extended narrative force. It seems possible, then, that the degree of difficulty depends on the degree to which the 'metaphoric' life of a poem takes over, or displaces, the poem's referents in the real world.

Our next poem, 'How shall my animal', is probably the most difficult of the three so far chosen. But don't worry too much as yet if it resists any easy paraphrase. However, given the hint that it deals with the problems of Thomas's poetry, try to clarify what in general terms it communicates to you on this subject. Also ask what you think causes the poem's *own* obscurity. Is it related to the kind of difficulty I mentioned in my last paragraph on 'The spire cranes'? How would you describe this poem's tone? Before moving on, and with these questions in mind, it would be helpful to read 'How shall my animal' two or three times. Indeed, reading aloud would be a help to get this longer poem's total effect:

> How shall my animal
> Whose wizard shape I trace in the cavernous skull,
> Vessel of abscesses and exultation's shell,
> Endure burial under the spelling wall,
> The invoked, shrouding veil at the cap of the face,
> Who should be furious,
> Drunk as a vineyard snail, flailed like an octopus,
> Roaring, crawling, quarrel
> With the outside weathers,
> The natural circle of the discovered skies
> Draw down to its weird eyes?

How shall it magnetize,
Towards the studded male in a bent, midnight blaze
That melts the lionhead's heel and horseshoe of the heart,
A brute land in the cool top of the country days
To trot with a loud mate the haybeds of a mile,
Love and labour and kill
In quick, sweet, cruel light till the locked ground sprout out,
The black, burst sea rejoice,
The bowels turn turtle,
Claw of the crabbed veins squeeze from each red particle
The parched and raging voice?

Fishermen of mermen
Creep and harp on the tide, sinking their charmed, bent pin
With bridebait of gold bread, I with a living skein,
Tongue and ear in the thread, angle the temple-bound
Curl-locked and animal cavepools of spells and bone,
Trace out a tentacle,
Nailed with an open eye, in the bowl of wounds and weed
To clasp my fury on ground
And clap its great blood down;
Never shall beast be born to atlas the few seas
Or poise the day on a horn.

Sigh long, clay cold, lie shorn,
Cast high, stunned on gilled stone; sly scissors ground in frost
Clack through the thicket of strength, love hewn in pillars drops
With carved bird, saint, and sun, the wrackspiked maiden mouth
Lops, as a bush plumed with flames, the rant of the fierce eye,
Clips short the gesture of breath.
Die in red feathers when the flying heaven's cut,
And roll with the knocked earth:
Lie dry, rest robbed, my beast.
You have kicked from a dark den, leaped up the whinnying light,
And dug your grave in my breast.
(p. 84)

DISCUSSION

You probably found yourself asking what evidence there is that the
poem is about Thomas's own poetry, or about poetry at all. After
all, we have been assailed with images of animal energy, and I would
agree that there seems little immediate evidence to point to all this
as metaphor. But I do think that the images which develop from
'animal' in the first line *are* metaphors: metaphors for the poet's inner
living experience, a kind of physical or sexual consciousness which
he wants to communicate in his verse. My interpretation is helped

when some line or other in the poem makes the literal subject (what it is, even if indirectly, about) appear momentarily through the metaphoric covering. In 'The spire cranes' I think you will agree that such a point of recognition came in the lines

> Those craning *birds* are choice for you, *songs* that jump back
> To the built voice

where the paralleling of 'birds' with 'songs' helps us see the equation. Therefore it is worth asking what lines from 'How shall my animal' would tend to support a similar equation.

I think the main suggestion comes conveniently early, in the first verse:

> How shall my animal . . .
> Endure burial under the spelling wall?

The 'spelling wall' is the poet's mouth, which *spells out* his inner experience in words. He laments the death which comes upon this experience when it is intellectually verbalized, reduced to mere words. He would like it to retain its dynamic energy, that energy which Thomas symbolizes in his various 'animal' images, an energy which he thinks is stultified or tamed when translated into words. The prose sense of the first verse might be outlined as follows. The poet asks how the mysterious physicality of his inner apprehension of experience can endure the death that will come upon it. He faintly traces it first of all in the head. The head is 'cavernous' because aware of the internal caverns in which this beast resides; but the head is in itself an inadequate 'vessel' or 'shell' for the mortal yet exultant life that the beast represents. How can it, then, 'endure' (*bear* or *survive*) the death represented by its verbalization? The mouth is a 'spelling wall' that merely memorializes past experience, or a 'shrouding veil at the cap of the face', obscuring what it seeks to express. This inner experience, to be true to itself, should rather retain its 'furious' energy. It should roar and crawl like the live thing it is. It should confront or 'quarrel' with the 'outside weathers' of external reality. That external world that we think of in such tidy, mastered ways ('the natural circle of the discovered skies') would then be 'drawn down' to a very different interpretation in the 'weird eyes' of the animal.

And yet one could imagine legitimate resistance to this particular reading. It would start by claiming that 'the spelling wall' could just as easily be a literal gravestone, and that the 'animal' that has to 'endure burial' is any dynamic form of life. Indeed, later images would seem to confirm the more literal 'gravestone' – notably 'the locked

ground', or the suggestions of a tombstone in 'love hewn in
pillars . . . With carved bird, saint, and sun', or the idea of a body
'rolling with the knocked earth'. But isn't the poem one in which
images breed other images? And surely the idea of potential material
for poetry being castrated by language, and that of life being trapped
by death, are in any case naturally cognate ones. But the primacy
of the language theme still has to be dictated by the poem, rather
than the critic. What other features, therefore, point up that reading?
Well, whatever the 'animal' is, it is internal – its 'wizard shape' is
'traced' in the mind ('the cavernous skull'). The poet 'angles' for it
there 'with a living skein,/Tongue and ear in the thread'. In being
brought out, the 'rant' of its 'fierce eye' is 'lopped' and the 'gesture'
of its 'breath' is 'clipped'. By what? By 'the wrack spiked maiden
mouth'. The very last line of the poem shows that any 'grave' involved
is still internal. The beast cannot be externalized. Thomas claimed
that bringing 'hidden causes' into 'the clean nakedness of light'[8] was
one of the aims of his poetry. In such an aim, it would appear that
he found obstacles not only in his own individual way with words
but also in what words are in the first place capable of expressing.
But, as we shall see, even that isn't the full extent of his quarrel with
language.

Given this initial clue as to theme, and as to what is also the main
nature of the poem's difficulty, you should consider whether, on re-
reading, you now find 'How shall my animal' as a whole clearer.
You should also test whether, along these lines, it makes *consistent*
sense. Any full paraphrase I offered here, however, would strike you
as being very thin compared to the dense original texture of the poem
itself; and your response should be to that texture, not to a dilute
paraphrase. You have seen that Thomas invests his energy, not in
a statement of ideas, but in a strong enactment of them through
images. He also obviously mixes his metaphors uncompromisingly.
The result is that each local part of the poem is not only texturally
dense, but constantly changing; from snail to octopus to horse, for
example; and notice how the associations of 'shorn', 'scissors', 'thicket
of strength' and 'pillars' in the last verse adds the Biblical Samson
to the list! It is worth quoting here Thomas's own description of his
poetic method: 'I make one image . . . let it breed another, let that
image contradict the first, make, of the third image bred out of the
other two together, a fourth contradictory image, and let them all,
within my imposed formal limits, conflict'.[9] We shall quote this
description more fully later, and raise more specifically his point
about this conflict of images being controlled 'within my imposed

formal limits'. In the present example, it is at least worth noting that, even while quickly changing, certain images seem to connect with one another even across the space of several lines. Is it possible, therefore, that the Samson images actually start with 'temple-bound' in the previous stanza?

Of course, you will have to decide for yourself whether you actually *like* the poem. One justification I would put forward for this wilful density (not just theoretically, but in relation to this specific poem's theme) is that it creates some impression of the very energies which Thomas says are usually tamed or castrated in words. Paradoxically, therefore, the poem is a victory over its own misgivings, and largely because Thomas has refused to reduce his theme to bare statement. With regard to my question about the poem's tone, I would argue also that it has a level of wit, a sense of verbal humour, which saves it from being merely a piece of muscle-bound helplessness. Thomas obviously delights in playing with words and images, and wants the reader to as well, without getting too solemnly hooked on direct or tidy meanings. And apart from this general exuberance there is the humour also of individual images. In verse 3, those other 'fishermen' who fish with a 'charmed, bent pin' and the 'bridebait of gold bread' are presumably other poets, interested in a less dynamic catch.

What do these three poems imply about the nature of the early poetry?

(a) It would seem that the poetry up to around 1938 had taken an unusual delight in language for its own sake. (Your experience of the later 'Fern Hill' (1945), however, will have suggested that Thomas wasn't to *over*-correct this.)

(b) It is also implied that, perhaps as a result of this delight in language, there had been an avoidance of more obviously human or humane subject-matter. (Your standard so far on this would be 'The Hunchback in the Park' which would seem to deny the implication. But though started early, that poem was indeed untypical of the earlier poetry, and was in any case freshly conceived in 1941.)

(c) It seems also that (despite what he claims to have been his relish for the autonomous effects of language) Thomas felt that the early poems were not spontaneous enough; that an analogy for their craft would be sculpture ('spire'), rather than music or painting. Added to this, there is even the implication in 'How shall my animal', that certain internal themes cannot survive verbalization.

(d) Lastly, there is an aspect of poetic method illustrated by these three poems themselves that we should be prepared for in coming to the early poetry. Thomas seems to have a natural tendency to translate the logic of his 'theme' immediately into a series of concrete images, which don't necessarily or obviously belong to it.

This last point suggests that Thomas often works by way of periphrasis, or circumlocution. In its simplest form, periphrasis is a kind of brief riddle, a local heightening of language (as when eighteenth-century poets call barley 'the bearded product', or fish 'the finny tribe', for example). But it is obviously something much more extensive in Thomas. After all, eighteenth-century poets don't pursue the 'bearded' properties of barley to the point where we have to make an effort to remember that it is barley we are concerned with! Similarly, in poetry of all kinds, what we normally call 'metaphor' has usually only a local life, in individual phrases. In Thomas, what is metaphorical in some way can often only be read as if 'literally', because it tends almost completely to replace the literal referent itself and to take on an extended life of its own. There are varying degrees to which he does this, so we shall still have to come back to the point to see if it is 'metaphor' in the normal sense that we are talking about.

All these points are indeed relevant to the textures and techniques of the earlier verse. But before we look at a range of examples from that period, in the next chapter, let us take one early poem ahead of time because, like the three poems from around 1938 that we have already looked at, it shows the same self-conscious concern with language itself as theme. It is 'Especially when the October wind', first published in 1934. An earlier version states its theme quite clearly. Especially during gusty autumn, the poet says,

> Does the brain reel, drunk on the raw
> Spirits of words, and the heart sicken
> Of arid syllables grouped and regrouped with care . . .[10]

In this more abstract earlier version, a clear distinction is drawn between rich experience-in-the-world and arid experience-via-language ('my heart rebells/Against the chain of words'). Now bearing that clarity of statement in mind, consider whether (or with what differences) the theme survives in the final poem. At the same time try to identify some examples of word-play that seem characteristic of Thomas's delight in complicating the local texture as well as the overall structure of a poem.

Especially when the October wind
With frosty fingers punishes my hair,
Caught by the crabbing sun I walk on fire
And cast a shadow crab upon the land,
By the sea's side, hearing the noise of birds,   5
Hearing the raven cough in winter sticks,
My busy heart who shudders as she talks
Sheds the syllabic blood and drains her words.

Shut, too, in a tower of words, I mark
On the horizon walking like the trees   10
The wordy shapes of women, and the rows
Of the star-gestured children in the park.
Some let me make you of the vowelled beeches,
Some of the oaken voices, from the roots
Of many a thorny shire tell you notes,   15
Some let me make you of the water's speeches.

Behind a pot of ferns the wagging clock
Tells me the hour's word, the neural meaning
Flies on the shafted disk, declaims the morning
And tells the windy weather in the cock.   20
Some let me make you of the meadow's signs;
The signal grass that tells me all I know
Breaks with the wormy winter through the eye.
Some let me tell you of the raven's sins.

Especially when the October wind   25
(Some let me make you of autumnal spells,
The spider-tongued, and the loud hill of Wales)
With fists of turnips punishes the land,
Some let me make you of the heartless words.
The heart is drained that, spelling in the scurry   30
Of chemic blood, warned of the coming fury.
By the sea's side hear the dark-vowelled birds.
(p. 15)

DISCUSSION

Consider the richness of some individual phrases first of all. The
'crabbing sun' (line 3) is both the less warm, *miserly* sun of October
and 'crabbing' because its light is sharp enough to cast the poet's crab-
like shadow. Similarly the casting of a shadow, as a primitive version
of photography, gives to 'caught' a photographic meaning, as in
caught the likeness of. Or take 'the rows of the star-gestured children
in the park' (line 12) where 'rows' is both *lines* and *quarrels*, and 'star-
gestured' suggests arms and legs outstretched, forming star-like
crosses. 'Autumnal spells' (line 26) are both magic spells and spells of

time or season. The multiple legs of a spider make 'spider-tongued' (line 27) remind us of the two languages and many accents of 'the loud hill of Wales'.

As to the main theme, Thomas has dropped the direct allusions to the aridity of language as associated with poetry. What he has done instead constitutes the main feature of the poem as it now stands. He has linked the concept of language to the substance, sight and significance of *things*. Thus we have 'the *wordy* shapes of women', 'the *vowelled* beeches', 'the oaken *voices*'. That association gives to the concept of language an integrity that language in the head, in the mouth, or on the page, doesn't have. Of course, he doesn't mean that these things actually speak, but that they have meaning – meaning that is not divorcible from their simple physical presence (a 'neural meaning'). And yet meaning is inconceivable without words. So if the reality of things won't cling to the words we use to name or describe them, the poet will attribute to things the power of meaning normally associated only with the status (and therefore the very terms) of language. Thus the circulation of his blood is controlled by a heart 'who shudders as she talks'. Thomas said 'When I experience anything I experience it as a thing and a word at the same time.'[11] We don't need as yet to identify complex reasons for this, beyond saying that it is likely to some degree to be a case of the attraction of words and the urge to be a poet being so intense that the two orders of reality (words and things) are constantly intermingling. But on the whole he seems to mistrust words more than things. Consider how even in this version whereas things *tell*, the poet himself offers not to tell, but to *make*. We have here perhaps a symbol of his choice in some poems of concrete enactment over discourse or description as the method for poetry. Concrete narratives create their own 'reality', while discourse or description tend to work by reflecting on the world as we already know it. Nevertheless, 'Especially when the October wind' itself still remains essentially a meditation on an actual world of recognizable things (October, trees, birds, grass etc.). It is closer to 'Once it was the colour of saying' than to 'How shall my animal' or 'The spire cranes'. But being, like these three, ultimately about language, it shows that that concern could be as self-consciously central in 1934 as in 1938.

Still, the concern with language did not take the form only of worry about what language can or cannot – or should – do. A far greater fear was that of not producing poetry at all. In another 1938 poem about his own poetry, he expressed his concern about not having produced new poems in the previous three months. The poem is 'On no work of words' (p. 87). I should like you to read it now with the following points in mind. It offers a serious argument concerning the poet's responsibilities. How would you describe this basic argument? In particular, what do you take Thomas to be saying in the last two lines of the poem? Paradoxically, he seems at the same time to be engaged in a good deal of witty word-play. To what would you point in illustrating this?

DISCUSSION

His 'three lean months' of non-productivity are contrasted with the fecundity of nature – and, self-satirically, with his own ample body. The colon at the end of the first verse shows that the meagreness of his output is taken 'to task' in relation to the three arguments given methodically in the remaining three verses: 'To take to give is all' (i.e. man's fullest responsibility is to return thanks for the created world in the form of creations of his own); 'To lift to leave' (i.e. to accept and then leave unused such gifts) is to please death; and 'To surrender now' (i.e. by not bothering about producing poems) is to pay death twice – in not bringing poems to birth and in his own final literal death.

The main difficulty at the end probably comes from the earlier of the last two lines:

Ancient woods of my blood, dash down to the nut of the seas
If I take to burn or return this world which is each man's work.

We wonder first of all what the image in that line is designed to evoke. We are also aware that it has to be both negative and positive, depending on whether the poet will 'burn' or 'return' this world. The negative idea in the image might be that of the 'woods' regressing to the 'nut' from which they grew. The significance of their being not just literal woods but 'woods of my blood' is that they evoke the evolutionary growth of humanity; hence the relevance of 'seas' – the source from which all life is taken to have emerged. The poet's failure to create is thus writ large in an image of the human world de-creating itself. The positive potential in the same image would be the idea of this being, not regression, but a return to the primary source ('the nut of the seas') for further growth. If these are broadly the two opposites evoked, notice how the pun on 'dash down' serves both meanings. 'Dash down' suggests both *breaking down* and *hurrying down*. And the poem ends on another kind of pun, created this time by ambiguity of syntax. I refer to the final clause – 'which is each man's work'. With 'return' as its subject, it means 'which is each man's duty'. But with 'world' as its subject, it says something philosophically more interesting: 'this world which is each man's work'. The point then would be that external reality is in a sense made by us, in our experience of it or our response to it. (Cf. Wordsworth – 'the mighty world/Of eye, and ear, – both what they half create,/And what perceive'.)[12] It is something that Thomas elsewhere stated explicitly about the specific role of poetry: 'A good poem is a contribution to reality. The world is never the same once a good poem has been added to it. A good poem helps to change the shape and significance of the universe, helps to extend everyone's knowledge of himself and the world around him'.[13]

The phenomenon we have encountered here, and in other poems in this chapter – the paradox of a poet saying in a good poem that good poetry is no longer possible for him – is in a long tradition stemming from the Romantic poets. One thinks immediately of Coleridge's 'Dejection: An Ode'. Or take Gerard Manley Hopkins:

> O then if in my lagging lines you miss
> The roll, the rise, the carol, the creation . . .

The last line beautifully manifests the very qualities it laments as no longer being possible. Indeed, the Hopkins poem (the sonnet 'To R[obert] B[ridges]') would be a good one to compare in greater detail with 'On no work of words'.

   This point about paradoxically wresting a new poem out of a poetic deadlock also highlights the sheer verbal inventiveness in Thomas's poem. You will no doubt have noticed the consistency with which financial images radiate from the word *rich* ('rich year') in the second line: 'purse', 'poverty', 'pounds', 'treasures', ['rake'], 'currencies', ['marked'], 'count', 'pay', 'expensive'. I have enclosed in square brackets words whose financial connotations come from the implied image of death as a croupier in a casino in the third verse. But also, I might have added the repeated words 'take' and 'give' – because in such company they, too, share in the same financial connotations. Likewise, the 'lean months' of the first verse. Though the phrase might evoke the 'lean years' of Pharaoh's dream in *Genesis* xli, it has the financial connotations also of simply having fallen on hard times. The line in the second verse,

   Puffing the pounds of manna up through the dew to heaven,

refers, of course, to God sending down manna to feed the hungry
Israelites, some of whom delayed partaking of the gift so that the
manna 'bred worms, and stank' (*Exodus* xvi). But notice that
Thomas attributes the hunger to God himself ('return what is *hungrily
given*') – as if God himself were hungry for a response. But there is
also another allusion in the line about the manna being puffed in
reverse to heaven. Its witty conceit probably came from George
Herbert's poem 'Prayer', where prayer is imaged as, amongst other
things, 'exalted manna' and 'reversed thunder'. Again, notice the
cliché 'gift of the gab' in the same verse: as in so many clichés, its
original metaphor (the *gift* of the gab) has gone dead; but this poem's
theme of returning what has been 'given' brings the dead metaphor
to life again. Thomas's use of the cliché isn't itself clichéd.
Nevertheless, it matches the suggestions of slang in some other
phrases, as in 'To lift to leave' for example. The aim of that phrase
is not only to parallel 'To take to give'; in slang terms, *to lift* is to
steal – a suitable meaning in a poem about 'taking' instead of
purchasing. Amidst so much verbal inventiveness, a suitable final
example can be the line

> I bitterly take to task my poverty and craft

'To take to task' in the sense of reprimanding, yes. To take to task
his 'craft' in the sense of poetic craft, yes. But also taken to task is
the *craftiness* of such excuses as he might find to salve his conscience
in the matter. That he *needs* to salve his conscience is suggested in
the ambiguity of a later phrase, when he says that 'to lift to
leave . . . is pleasing death': *is to please death*, yes; but also *is a
pleasing death*. The man, who so often in his letters described the
writing of poetry as unbearably hard work, knew as well as anyone
the pleasure of being released from its demands. But nevertheless
another meaning in 'to take to task' is to take *to* the task – the task
of writing this poem. And the verbal inventiveness we have seen here
in his return to that task is something we should continue to keep
an eye on in turning now to his early poetry.

3. The Early Poetry

We have become used to difficulty, if not downright obscurity, in a good deal of modern poetry; so it comes as no surprise to discover these traits in Thomas's early poems. But it has to be said at once that Thomas's poetry is difficult and obscure in an individual way; and the five poems we have looked at so far will have suggested this. Quite often, the early poems may seem to offer the reader only an impenetrable enigma. It is not, as with Eliot, a question of allusions to other works of literature that you need to track down; or, as with Yeats, a case of a poem beginning from some fairly accessible experience or emotion, but taking the reader on a journey into deeply mysterious territories. The problem often seems one of not knowing where a poem begins to engage a recognizable world of experience other than itself. Thomas will seem to make up a new language, using words, phrases and grammar altogether familiar in themselves, but positively arranged in a new way. Perhaps the nearest analogy, though not one I would want to push too far, is to a secret code, whose rules have to be deciphered from the coded messages alone. Discussion of these poems will inevitably, then, involve some preliminary 'decoding', and a part of my comment will take that form.

But before examining any poem in detail, I'd like you to read a few for yourself, and see what you make of them. Don't worry at this stage how much, or how little, you manage to understand. Remember Eliot's remark that poetry often communicates *before* it is understood.[1] At least you will be able to judge whether a poem attracts you sufficiently to determine its meaning more fully, and any attraction of this sort will remain an important part of the poem's achievement and power. Ask yourself what general impressions you have of these poems. What is the poet's tone of voice? He writes directly about his own experience, the words 'I' and 'my' occurring frequently. Can you glean anything of what he is saying about it? Or again, what sort of language does he use? Lyrical? Descriptive? And what of the rhythm, and generally the shape of each poem? Where do you find examples of the punning word-play we anticipated in the last chapter? Keeping these questions in mind, please read now 'The force that through the green fuse drives the flower' (p. 8), 'When once the twilight locks no longer' (p. 3), 'A process in the weather of the heart' (p. 5), and 'Light breaks where no sun shines' (p. 21). These, incidentally, were some of the *18 Poems* with which Thomas broke upon an admiring if also astonished literary world in 1934. Imagine yourself in the situation of those first readers, even the first reviewers, who can hardly have understood the poems as we, with the advantage of time and study, are in a position to understand them. A major critic, William Empson, recalls his contemporary impression of such poems as being 'overwhelmingly good, though one resisted them because one couldn't see why', claiming that 'they hit you before you know how'.[2] Consider what qualities might account for that impression, and what part is played in it by the kind of themes evoked.

DISCUSSION

My own general impressions are as follows:

(a) The poems are built around emphatic but riddlingly mysterious statements, repeated and varied with the effect of a refrain. Thus:

   (i) A process in the weather of the heart
        Turns damp to dry . . .
        A process in the weather of the world
        Turns ghost to ghost . . .

  (ii) The force that through the green fuse drives the flower
        Drives my green age . . .
        The hand that whirls the water in the pool
        Stirs the quicksand . . .

 (iii) When once the twilight locks no longer
        Locked in the long worm of my finger . . .
        When the galactic sea was sucked
        And all the dry seabed unlocked . . .

 (iv) Light breaks where no sun shines;
        Where no sea runs, the waters of the heart
        Push in their tides . . .

It is as if the incantational, 'reminding' effect we associate with traditional refrains, instead of being isolated in final lines, has been diffused through the body of the stanzas themselves. Our sense of consistent wholeness probably comes more from these repeated syntactic forms than from connections between individual words or images or from our grasp of overall theme; certainly on a first encounter.

(b) The rhythms are strongly marked, and the stanzas given firm shapes, with a clear pattern of rhymes and (mainly) half-rhymes. This point is closely connected with (a), since the stanzas develop out of the kind of sentences I've just quoted. Repetition and firm shapes, then, give the impression of a few primary moods and ideas being locked in, perpetuated, dwelt upon. This is certainly not a casual, free-wheeling voice. There is a sense of strikingly active language being contained by an almost sculptural attention to shapes and forms – and (less obviously) by a patterned count of the number of syllables per line. You might now check some examples. Thus in 'Light breaks where no sun shines' the number of syllables per line within each verse follows the pattern: 6, 10, 4, 10, 4, 10. What patterns do you find in the other poems?

(c) The poet's tone is eloquent, heightened, authoritative, grave. It is curiously 'bardic', even impersonal in a way, and I think one is affected by prophetic tones more than by any impression of a developing statement. Biblical prose rhythms would seem to be an influence (essentially familiar ones like 'And God said, "Let there be Light, and there was Light"' – from *Genesis*).

(d) The poems seem to describe, or to report on, *processes* (consider the number of verbs of energetic action: 'drives', 'whirls'; 'breaks', 'push'), and one has the sense of primal, elemental energies. The processes refer, at one and the same time, outwardly to nature's activities ('weather', 'water', 'twilight', 'sun', 'tides', etc.), and inwardly to events in the poet's own body ('blood', 'nerve', 'brain', 'heart'). The effect is to bring the two into intimate, but mysterious, connection.

I'd like now to look in rather more detail at three of these poems. Please re-read carefully first of all 'The force that through the green fuse' (p. 8). What does it add up to? Can you say what it is about? Where does it seem clear, and where difficult? What do you make of the contrast between the first three verses and the fourth?

There is, by the way, a punctuation mistake in the second verse of your text:

> And I am dumb to mouth unto my veins.
> How at the mountain spring the same mouth sucks.

The full-stop after 'veins' is clearly wrong. Keep a look out for this kind of misprint.

DISCUSSION

A few details apart, the poem is fairly straightforward. The poet claims that the energies of the universe and those by which he lives are identical. The point is made, with variations, in each verse. The first verse refers to flowers and trees, the second to mountains and rivers, the third to water, wind and sand, the fourth to the stars – so that the perspective expands to embrace the whole universe. Each verse also expresses the poet's inability to express this truth, as if it were so vast and overwhelming as to be beyond words. Or is it because, unlike the rose or his own veins or the wind, only he has to use the medium of language in the first place? So what can we say this adds up to? A statement about the unity of human and natural life? True to an extent – and the conflation works by depersonalizing the human body while personalizing the body of the world. But surely the tone also suggests something more than that – a desire to speak, to 'tell', which is continually frustrated, leaving the poet in some sense cut off from the very things with which he nevertheless identifies.

The fourth verse seems to me more obscure than the others:

> The lips of time leech to the fountain head;
> Love drips and gathers, but the fallen blood
> Shall calm her sores.
> And I am dumb to tell a weather's wind
> How time has ticked a heaven round the stars.

Did you notice that it doesn't use the syntactic formula whereby the previous stanzas had claimed that '*the force that does A also does B*'? Is it possible, therefore, that the first three lines here combine an outward and an inner event without so obviously showing that it is doing so? The lines certainly suggest to me an image of birth. Thus time sucks the child from the 'fountain head' of the womb, and the 'fallen blood' of a painful birth heals the mother. Thomas now allows the literal and the metaphoric meanings of 'fountain head' to combine without comment, with a more mysterious assertiveness. If we turn to the last two lines of the same verse, they seem to me to hint at the poem's religious limits. It is time, and the pressure of time, Thomas seems to be saying, that has caused man fancifully

The Young Poet
Acknowledgement: Pamela Hansford Johnson (Lady Snow)

to invent the concept of 'heaven' or eternity (the last line originally read, simply, 'How time is all' – all-important, and all there is).[3] I at least think this reading accords with the general tone of the poem, with its acceptance of physical, rather than spiritual, truths.

Two general points about the language are worth making. First, the occasional, brilliantly unexpected choice of a single word. Take the first line. What does 'fuse' mean? There seems nothing in the organic world to refer it to. One would expect the force of natural energy to drive the flower through a system of roots and stems. 'Fuse' suggests electricity and (more precisely – because of 'blasts' in the next line) the combustible strip used to ignite a bomb. So, by attraction, 'force' is given a modern scientific connotation, and any vaguely Wordsworthian possibilities are avoided. This relates to my second point – the deliberate use of multiple meanings, which you will now have recognized as a regular feature of the poems. Thus in the third verse the effect of 'whirls' and 'stirs' makes 'quicksand' also suggest the draining action of sand in an hourglass. And the 'quick' in 'quicksand' also links with the 'hangman's lime' at the end of that verse, because the lime in which the bodies of convicts are disposed is of course *quicklime*. Or look at the last verse. The 'lover's tomb' is the bed as well as the grave since 'crooked worm' suggests sexuality as well as death. In that case, 'sheet' evokes bedclothes as well as burial-sheets. And possibly even a third meaning comes into play, with the 'crooked worm' suggesting the finger of the poet's hand writing on his 'sheet' of paper. The physical act of writing shouldn't surprise us as a meaning here. The same self-consciousness occurs in an early short story, 'The Orchards': 'He raised his pencil so that its shadow fell, a tower of wood and lead, on the clean paper; he fingered the pencil tower, the half-moon of his thumb-nail rising and setting behind the leaden spire. The tower fell, down fell the city of words, the walls of a poem, the symmetrical letters'.[4] I think the activation of multiple meanings in so many parts warrants our also considering another meaning for 'dumb' in 'dumb to tell': 'dumb' in the colloquial sense of *foolish*. It confirms the feeling that language only rationalizes a relationship between inner and outer that is already known at deeper organic levels. Of course, each reader must decide as to which readings are legitimately read out of a phrase. Your best guide each time is your own impression of the areas of experience a poem points to, and the general kind of verbal virtuosity it shows. On that score, what do you yourself think of this poem? I would be surprised if you remained indifferent to it.

Now re-read carefully 'Light breaks where no sun shines' (p. 21) with the same points in mind. Is the poem saying the same kind of thing as

'The force that through . . .'? How are the two poems related? A
clue to reading the poem is to take the lines as literally as possible.
Thus, what kind of light could break 'where no sun shines'?

DISCUSSION

Again, Thomas is evoking a close identity between the events of
nature and events within the human body. His physical organic life
is given a kind of elemental grandeur by such lines as

> Dawn breaks behind the eyes;
> From poles of skull and toe the windy blood
> Slides like a sea.

'Windy' seems to me another of those brilliantly unexpected words,
identifying the circulation of the blood with the movement of the
sea round the globe; and again 'slides' conveys a vivid physical effect
of process. More mysteriously, the lines

> Night in the sockets rounds,
> Like some pitch moon, the limit of the globes

suggest not only a cosmic darkness in the eye-sockets but at the same
time a kind of Alice-through-the-Looking-Glass world where
darkness is light, and the moon gives off darkness. Again, the effect
is to suggest the mystery and grandeur of the physical life. And of
death, too: 'Where no wax is, the candle shows its hairs'; notice the
play on 'wax' in the sense of *growth*.

The poem differs from 'That force that through . . .', I think,
in that the latter keeps body and universe separate (remember the
theme of being 'dumb to tell'), though giving both a common, linking
energy. In 'Light breaks where no sun shines' the two are identified,
intermingled, each taking the character of the other, with only two
actual statements of comparison. These are the similes 'slides like
a sea' and 'like some pitch moon': the rest of the poem doesn't say
that A is like B, but that A *is* B.

Did you decide what kind of light Thomas refers to in the poem's
opening line? 'Light' here surely draws on a familiar metaphorical
usage: the light of reason or understanding (as we might say, *it
dawned on me*). But Thomas seems to want to reduce the feeling
of it being a mere metaphor. He also makes it something tougher
than a riddle. Such light breaks where no sun shines, not in the
external universe, but in the head. But the last verse makes an
important distinction between a kind of physically-based consciousness
and rational 'logic'. In death 'logics die', and man's only life then

is the life that his body now quite literally shares with nature ('the secret of the soil' growing literally 'through the eye'). But this isn't extinction. In death, the 'dawn' of organic consciousness 'halts'. That is, it *remains*. We shall return later to consider the value of such an idea, *as* an idea. At present it is useful to ask 'What?' rather than 'So what?'

We get the impression, then, of poems struggling to celebrate inchoate elemental states which normally lie beyond or beneath the articulation of civilized language. In this sense, 'How shall my animal' seems an accurate reflection of the preoccupations, and attendant difficulties, of the early verse. This kind of poetry certainly doesn't present ideas *as* ideas, and there is a determined avoidance of abstract language. And yet, at the same time, I wonder if you feel that 'Once it was the colour of saying' could, in one way, have wrongly prepared us for what we have now found. Obviously, descriptions such as 'the colour of saying' and 'the gentle seaslides of saying' quite accurately apply to the way in which words are individually relished for their musical sound as well as sense. (And of course, it is another effect of a word's sound that makes puns possible.) Yet we surely also feel that each poem so far has been decidedly *about* something, and has a strong *narrative* movement. There has been much in modern English and continental poetry since the late nineteenth century that has drawn on the 'Symbolist' aim of making poetry aspire to the condition of music. As it happens, this was only one of many impulses to make modern poetry avoid discourse, or mere description. Yet even in the extreme case of Mallarmé, the notion that a poem need not be 'about anything' is finally a simplification, even if we only say that it relates to human experience. My point, however, is that Thomas seems directly and busily *descriptive*, even while he preserves his own characteristic degree of mystery. The incantational music may momentarily postpone a question like 'What is all this about?' But in the end the reader wants to (and can) do something more rational with this poetry than simply 'sucking it in through his pores'.[5] The difficulty you are likely to encounter in the early poems has more to do with the strangeness of the material (e.g. prenatal life) or with syntactical obscurity, or with resisting your temptation to reduce a poem completely into terms other than the ones actually used, than with any decision on the poet's part to abandon himself to mere mood-music, or automatic writing.

The early poems looked at so far have not presented serious difffculties of syntax. Such difficulties tend to arise when Thomas is bent on building up a long series of auxiliary clauses and

appositional phrases. This has not been the case in the examples
chosen so far from the early poems, but 'How shall my animal' from
our last chapter will have prepared you for the kind of difficulty
involved. Here is an example from an early poem, 'I, in my intricate
image' (p. 30):

> I, in my intricate image, stride on two levels,
> Forged in man's minerals, the brassy orator
> Laying my ghost in metal,
> The scales of this twin world tread on the double,
> My half ghost in armour hold hard in death's corridor,
> To my man-iron sidle.

Here, the opening 'I' is in fact the subject of all the following verbs:
'stride', 'tread', 'hold', and 'sidle'. But you can see how easily one
can start imagining other syntactic possibilities. In the fourth line,
for example, 'scales' might be taken (wrongly) to be the subject of
'tread'. Almost the first thing one should do with the densest of the
early poems is work out the syntax. We shall encounter some other
examples as we proceed, and also return to the general subject of
syntax in our final chapter.

   I also mentioned above the danger of the reader reducing an
early poem into terms other than the ones the poem actually uses.
An example from 'Light breaks where no sun shines' even led Thomas
into a comic misunderstanding involving the BBC. Think back to
the lines

> Nor fenced, nor staked, the gushers of the sky
> Spout to the rod
> Divining in a smile the oil of tears.

The poem's publication in the BBC's *The Listener* led to letters
of protest about what was taken to be the phallic nature of the
image. 'The little smut-hounds', said Thomas, 'thought I was
writing a copulatory anthem. In reality, of course, it was a metaphysical image of rain and grief'.[6] One can see that the phallic
interpretation is certainly wrong here (whereas it wouldn't be in
the poem's second verse, if you look at it). But the example is
useful in pointing to a far greater danger: that of paraphrasing
Thomas's images in ways that take *no account at all* of the
words actually used. Readers of *The Listener* had at least responded
to the concreteness of *gushers*, *spout*, and *rod* (though they
seem obviously to have denied the same actuality to *tears*). In
the next chapter we shall see an example of a reading of another
poem that paraphrases its images out of existence. (See below,
p. 56).

Let us now look more closely at the third of our poems. Please re-read 'When once the twilight locks no longer' (p. 3). Try to decide what the relation is of the 'I' and 'he' of the poem. Ask yourself in what way, and through what stages, the poem develops. Where does it seem to you most difficult? Your reading should be a preparation for saying broadly what it is 'about', but again as far as possible without betraying the demands made by the concreteness of the actual language used.

DISCUSSION

I shall quote various stanzas of the poem as I discuss them. It opens, you'll remember, like this:

> *as soon as*
> When once the twilight locks no longer
> Locked in the long worm of my finger
> Nor damned the sea that sped about my fist,
> The mouth of time sucked, like a sponge,
> The milky acid on each hinge,   5
> And swallowed dry the waters of the breast.
>
> When the galactic sea was sucked
> And all the dry seabed unlocked,
> I sent my creature scouting on the globe,
> That globe itself of hair and bone   10
> That, sewn to me by nerve and brain,
> Had stringed my flask of matter to his rib.

mad / universe

My experience in the first three lines is of several accidental syntactical possibilities occurring to my ear, even though the main syntax is quite specific. Thus 'locks' is a noun, not a verb; the verb is 'locked in'. Even 'When once' might first of all suggest *When once upon a time*; but what it clearly has to mean is *as soon as*. At this stage one is any case not clear as to what event is being described. But lines 4–6 clearly suggest an infant suckling at the breast. This is the clue to the first three lines, which evoke the stage following birth – when the baby and the amniotic fluid ('the sea that sped about my fist') are no longer locked in by the twilight of the womb. You can see my point about not betraying the actual language used: my talk of baby, birth and suckling is decidedly sentimental compared to Thomas's 'locks', 'worm', 'sponge', 'hinge' and 'waters'.

Verse two shows that the speaker is not a simple, or single, identity. 'Creature' suggests the physical child being described by his own inner, spiritual or mental, consciousness. (cf. 'And time cast forth my mortal creature' in the poem 'Before I knocked'.) This makes

sense because the creature is 'sewn' to the speaker by nerve and brain,
the organs of sensation and consciousness. Notice how the idea of
'sewn' is kept physical in 'stringed': the more accurate 'strung' would
also have been more abstract. At this stage, however, meanings are
still tentative. For example, is the 'globe' which the creature explores
(1.9) that of the outside world? It seems also an exploration of his
own body – described as a 'globe itself of hair and bone'.
Furthermore, the idea occurs that the poem *might* be an address by
God, the creature being the human being He created. However, I
don't feel I've missed the essential drift of the lines. This seems mainly
because the strong narrative insistence of the lines creates a sense
of release and adventure that is not immediately dependent on my
recognizing exact identities.
    Then:

> My fuses timed to charge his heart,
> He blew like powder to the light
> And held a little sabbath with the sun,   15
> But when the stars, assuming shape, *growing up*
> Drew in his eyes the straws of sleep,
> He drowned his father's magics in a dream. *views*

This *third verse* makes me feel that for the first time certain value-
judgements are coming into play. The creature so dynamically sent
into the world of light (contrast the 'twilight' of the womb) celebrates
that world only momentarily – 'held a little sabbath with the sun'.
Instead, he surrenders himself more enthusiastically to the world of
night, sleep, and dreams. One is unsure at this stage as to what 'his
father's magics' might be; or whether 'sabbath' and 'father' again
suggest that the speaker is God; and it even occurs to me that the
speaker may be the literal father or mother. We should discount,
however, both God and parent as speaker by remembering that the
speaker has to be the same as the baby of the opening stanza ('the
sea that sped about *my* fist'). Characteristically, certain words seem
to spark off each other. 'Sabbath' half evokes Sunday out of the word
'sun'. 'Drew . . . the straws of sleep' evokes the idea of *drawing lots* – a
meaning that is confirmed three verses later by the line 'By trick *or
chance* he fell asleep'.
    Then we come to these two verses:

> All issue armoured of the grave,
> The redhaired cancer still alive,   20
> The cataracted eyes that filmed their cloth;
> Some dead undid their bushy jaws,
> And bags of blood let out their flies;
> He had by heart the Christ-cross-row of death.

Sleep navigates the tides of time;   25
The dry Sargasso of the tomb
Gives up its dead to such a working sea;
And sleep rolls mute above the beds
Where fishes' food is fed the shades
Who periscope through flowers to the sky.   30

An immediate impression of diseased death is powerfully felt in the
very texture of the language, especially in lines 21–23. I take it,
however, that these two verses are the most likely to create difficulty.
The last word of the previous verse was 'dream'. Here, then, Thomas
is giving a vivid enactment of that dream. It is as if the imagination
had surrendered itself to a morbid fantasy-world of subconscious
nightmare. One wonders: does Thomas mean a literal dream or
simply the workings of a conscious but morbid imagination? I think
it is the latter, and that the phase of development implied is that
of adolescence. And what about the phrase 'Christ-cross-row of
death' (l.24)? It communicates without our going to the dictionary,
certainly. It first suggested to me, for example, a row of graves in
a graveyard. As it happens, the dictionary tells us that 'Christ-cross-
row' means the alphabet (a cross was placed before a row of letters
in early spelling-books). Possibly, therefore, Thomas partly thinks
of the 'dream' as being the morbid tendencies of his own poetry,
reflecting as it often did the murky sensibility of adolescence.

But these questions, and even doubts about the exact identity
of the speaker, don't radically obscure the poem's main statement.
This is memorably climaxed in the last verse. (The penultimate verse
is simply a recapitulation of the first five verses.) The creature ('my
sleeper') is urged to commit himself not to the morbid world of
adolescent dreams and fears but to the waking everyday world of
reality. In that case, what he had done when he 'drowned his father's
magics in a dream' (l.18) was betray, not only the magic process
of his begetting, but the normal healthy world that a parent would
want him to be heir to. (An earlier version of that line about
drowning his father's magics was 'He doublecrossed his getter with
a dream'.)[7] The 'worlds' which hang on the trees in the last line are
therefore the worlds of promise and achievement, which lie outside
the globe of his own body and his own subconscious:

Awake, my sleeper, to the sun,
A worker in the morning town,
And leave the poppied pickthank where he lies;
The fences of the light are down,
All but the briskest riders thrown,
And worlds hang on the trees.

Now consider for a moment what you would say is the main difference between 'When once the twilight' and the other poems we have read in this chapter. Since substantially it seems to use similar material, you will understand that I am drawing attention more to the way in which it develops, and the use to which its characteristic material is put.

'When once the twilight' seems to me more self-possessed, developing more obviously towards an assertive resolution. In this it has something of a traditional moral shape. Compare the relatively static quality of 'The force that through . . .' or 'Light breaks where no sun shines', at least in terms of developing statement. Though I personally like all the poems we've looked at so far, I have also admitted that with some of them one is likely to ask not only 'What?' but 'So what?' Something that seems to me significant about 'When once the twilight locks no longer', therefore, is the fact that Thomas *is* capable of some measure of self-scrutiny and self-appraisal. The poem, surely ultimately about himself, is outwardly analytical as well as murkily self-revelatory. One could even see verses four and five as self-parody of what he takes to be his own usual obsession with death and decay. Some such quality of poise and reflection helps the poem fuse what Eliot called 'the most ancient and the most civilized mentality'.[8]

For this reason, I think a new reader should not learn to expect only poems of 'primitive' utterance about elemental processes in the early phase of Thomas's career. Accordingly, I would like you now to look at eight poems of a different kind. I don't mean that they are linguistically different. I have selected them because I think they are more obviously meditative poems. Simply test in this first reading how quickly you grasp the essential theme of each poem. Don't worry if any part or phrase proves difficult; you can come back to the poems again later. Arrange the poems in your mind by considering the following questions.

(a) All but three start with a sufficiently 'open' meditative language and put us quite quickly in possession of theme. Which are the three exceptions?

(b) Three are on what we might call more 'public' themes than we have encountered so far. Which three?

(c) One seems fairly close to 'When once the twilight locks no longer'. Which one?

(d) Which two seem to you to have very much the same theme?

These are the poems, mainly short ones, which you should now please read: 'This bread I break' (p. 34), 'Out of the sighs' (p. 43), 'Why east wind chills' (p. 48), 'Ears in the turrets hear' (p. 53), 'The hand that signed the paper' (p. 56), 'Should lanterns shine' (p. 57), 'I have longed to move away' (p. 58), 'Our eunuch dreams' (p. 13).

DISCUSSION

Taking the questions in order, here are my comments on them:

(a) I think that with the majority of these poems we feel, from the start, that they engage recognizable subjects, moods, or ideas. In other words, we obviously find our bearings quite quickly with a poem which starts with lines such as:

> Out of the sighs a little comes,
> But not of grief . . .

or such as this:

> This bread I break was once the oat,
> This wine upon a foreign tree
> Plunged in its fruit . . .

There is, after all, no way in which even Dylan Thomas could completely detach sighs or grief, or the breaking of bread, from their usual meanings in the real world. In this sense, the three exceptions are 'Our eunuch dreams', 'Ears in the turrets hear', and 'Should lanterns shine' – because they open with an uncompromising imagistic narrative which makes us more aware of things and images than of statements. Yet these three poems are by no means equally difficult. 'Ears in the turrets hear', for example, is soon felt to be a simple meditation on the poet's responsibility to accommodate a world of adult experience outside the 'bone coast' of his own body. (Is that how you read it?) And 'Should lanterns shine' opens out into a more orthodox discursive style after its first verse. 'Our eunuch dreams' is surely the one that maintains most consistently the density of the other early poems we looked at. (Incidentally, 'Our eunuch dreams' is the only one, in this present group, from *18 Poems*. The others are from Thomas's second volume *Twenty-Five Poems* (1936). But this should not too quickly suggest a changing style. Thomas's first three volumes all drew heavily on poems already present in his Notebooks of 1930–1934.)

(b) By 'public' themes I meant to suggest material which is at least at some remove from the world of organic process or from a confessional private emotion. Obviously, this distinction is not a simple matter in Thomas's case, especially in the early poetry. 'The hand that signed the paper', dealing with the nature of tyranny, is unusually 'public' for Thomas. Indeed, it is his only overtly 'political' poem, a fact that reminds us how much Thomas's obsession with organic processes as theme must have contrasted with the Marxicising poetic fashions of the 1930s. More characteristically, 'This bread I break' is concerned with the vital forces in nature which produce wine and bread, and thus might even invite some comparison with, say, 'The force that through the green fuse . . .' But I'm sure you'll agree that 'This bread I break' is also organized in relation to a decidedly 'public' concept: the ritual of the Holy Communion. Thomas here seems intellectually challenged by the paradox that the life-giving emblems of the Eucharist are produced by ending their life in nature, as oat and grape. The central idea here seems, if anything, more challenging and discussable than any equivalent idea in 'The force that through . . .'

   'Our eunuch dreams' also engages a public (one might even say 'social') theme. Thomas condemns the suppressed sexuality which is forced to find its satisfaction in deathly erotic dreams (Section I), and also – a more surprising theme – condemns the fictionally glamorous images of cinema films (Section II). Both kinds of escapism are unreal, he urges, and deprive us of 'faith' in ordinary reality.

(c) It is 'Our eunuch dreams', then, that should remind us of 'When once the twilight locks no longer'. Both urge an engagement with the real world, as opposed to life-denying dreams. Yet the use of the extended cinema references here is obviously less private than anything in 'When once the twilight':

> In this our age the gunman and his moll,
> Two one-dimensioned ghosts, love on a reel,
> Strange to our solid eye,
> And speak their midnight nothings as they swell;
> When cameras shut they hurry to their hole
> Down in the yard of day.
>
> They dance between their arclamps and our skull,
> Impose their shots, throwing the nights away;
> We watch the show of shadows kiss or kill,
> Flavoured of celluloid give love the lie.
> (p. 13)

The usual surface difficulties or richnesses are there. Thus in 'love on a reel', in the second line 'love' is a main verb though it might register with us first of all as a noun. And 'swell' in line 4 characteristically suggests three meanings at once: sexual tumescence is suggested as well as that the images on the screen *grow larger than life* and *show off*. But the recognizability of the theme is matched by a relatively direct presentation. It would be useful, however, to compare the section with the three opening stanzas of C. Day Lewis's 'Newsreel', a poem on the same theme from the same period. Ask yourself what the essential differences are. Here is C. Day Lewis:

> Enter the dream-house, brothers and sisters, leaving
> Your debts asleep, your history at the door:
> This is the home for heroes, and this loving
> Darkness a fur you can afford.
>
> Fish in their tanks electrically heated
> Nose without envy the glass wall: for them
> Clerk, spy, nurse, killer, prince, the great and the defeated,
> Move in a mute day-dream.
>
> Bathed in this common source, you gape incurious
> At what your active hours have willed –
> Sleep-walking on that silver wall, the furious
> Sick shapes and pregnant fancies of your world.[9]

Would you agree that the main difference comes from the fact that Day Lewis chooses factual 'newsreel' rather than fictional film? His concern is with how the cinema can warp *political* consciousness. As a result, his poem is 'public' in a more detailed way than anything we could imagine from Thomas. The capacity of cinema to deceive is the same in both and is attacked by both as a form of dream, but the external world from which Day Lewis launches his attack seems more genuinely present. Thomas invests his energy instead in elaborating the very thing that he urges is insubstantial! There is an imaginative relish in the two Thomas stanzas quoted above which is reinforced later in the poem:

> The photograph is married to the eye,
> Grafts on its bride one-sided skins of truth;
>
> . . . our shots shall smack
> The image from the plates;

That is rather like Dickens saying of Miss Tox in *Dombey and Son* that she looks at people 'as if she were mentally engaged in taking off impressions of their images upon her soul'.[10] The very concreteness of the presentation reminds us how solidly Thomas adheres to his metaphors. And the converse of this is how insubstantial is the celebration of the real world into which he wishes to be freed. After detailing the society weddings, the 'hysteric treble' of warplanes, the 'rags of children' in the rest of his poem, Day Lewis says simply to his deceived brothers and sisters at the end 'You'll know you slept too long'. The logic of the 'public' nature of his theme brings Thomas, however, to a vaguer concluding gesture (reminiscent of the similar final stanza of 'When once the twilight'):

> And who remain shall flower as they love,
> Praise to our faring hearts.

This is not necessarily to say that it is an insincere or meaningless gesture. What it shows is that, even to more 'open' or 'public' themes, Thomas at this stage brings the same tendencies and techniques as serve more private materials.

I suggested – question (d) above – that two of these poems are close in theme, and we shall end this first look at the early poetry with them. Conveniently so, because I think they memorably evoke Thomas's philosophical position – though, as you will see, 'philosophical' is not quite the right word. The two poems are 'Should lanterns shine' and 'Why east wind chills'. Please re-read both poems now, asking yourself again what theme, and what images, are common to both. Which of the two, for you, is the richer treatment?

DISCUSSION

For convenience, I shall print 'Should lanterns shine' here, and you should take as your starting-point the question as to what idea you think Thomas wants to communicate in its opening verse. What sense do you make of individual words or phrases such as 'octagon' and 'false day'? There seems to be a change of style between the first and second verse: what ideas do you think establish nevertheless a connection between them?

> Should lanterns shine, the holy face,
> Caught in an octagon of unaccustomed light,
> Would wither up, and any boy of love
> Look twice before he fell from grace.
> The features in their private dark
> Are formed of flesh, but let the false day come
> And from her lips the faded pigments fall,
> The mummy cloths expose an ancient breast.
>
> I have been told to reason by the heart,
> But heart, like head, leads helplessly;
> I have been told to reason by the pulse,
> And, when it quickens, alter the actions' pace

Till field and roof lie level and the same
So fast I move defying time, the quiet gentleman
Whose beard wags in Egyptian wind.

I have heard many years of telling,
And many years should see some change.

The ball I threw while playing in the park
Has not yet reached the ground.
(p. 57)

That first verse develops a dense concrete image, sustained in a way that makes us feel that it embodies a complete idea. Again, the conditional 'Should' prepares us for an implied argument, not just a narrative. And yet the abstract outline of an argument ('Should . . . Would . . . but . . .') links incorrigibly concrete details rather than abstract statements. The idea that certain evaluative judgements are being made is evoked in key words, but words that still cannot be detached from the concrete narrative itself: 'holy face', 'wither up', 'boy of love', 'fell from grave', 'private dark', 'false day', 'expose'. Looking further at the structural development of the whole poem, it is useful to discover its logical shape before deciding on specific meanings. The shape may strike us at first as *il*logical. The second verse may appear a *non-sequitur* in relation to the first, at least until it reaches an 'Egyptian' image that picks up the associations of 'mummy cloths' in the opening verse. In itself, however, the second verse seems reasonably clear. Several approaches to life have been urged on the poet ('I have been told to . . .'). Yet why the repeated emphasis on 'reason' – used in connection with 'heart' and 'pulse' as well as 'head'? But at least the penultimate couplet follows from that second verse: he has been 'told' many things – which have neither changed things nor themselves been changed. Then the final couplet introduces a completely different concrete image – a ball thrown in a childhood park.

Lest we assume too easily that the switch in idiom between the first two verses is simply a case of the poet's being unsure of the effect he's after, let us try to see whether the second verse might not have developed quite logically out of the first. It seems odd that the powers of the mind should be so briefly referred to – 'like head' – almost as a mere aside. But what if it isn't a mere aside, but a reference back to the real meaning of the whole image in the opening verse? The image itself is that of opening up a tomb, and surely what it comes to represent is man's use of his rational faculties in seeking to penetrate mystery. What the 'lanterns' of rational or scientific enquiry would bring to the tomb would be a 'false day' – not a real daylight or a day of real revelation. (The light is octagonal because of either the shape of the lantern's aperture or the shape of the tomb itself.) The artificial light of empirical reason causes the object of its discovery (metaphorically, the mummy's 'holy face') to 'wither up'. Any 'boy of love' would 'look twice' (cf. *think twice*) before falling 'from grace' – into (metaphorically) necrophilia or (literally) a betrayal of the respect for mystery that is necessary to life. This mistrust of presumptuous reason matches the poet's dismissal also of an emotional philosophy of the 'heart' and a physical philosophy of the 'pulse', such as perhaps D. H. Lawrence would advocate. In the latter case the presumption is that of trying to conquer time by racing it. Time itself takes its time: that 'quiet gentleman's' beard still 'wags in Egyptian wind'. The poem's point is surely that any self-conscious attempt to explain or master life will falsify the very thing it is exploring. It seems to urge instead a simple, open acceptance of experience and its mystery. A wise passiveness of this kind is suggested by the very tone of the final image of the ball thrown in the park, which is why perhaps we shouldn't too actively try to unpack or fix its meaning. But we surely also sense its logic. The ball 'has not yet reached the ground' because life is still in play, celebrated by the imagination rather than analysed by the reason, sentimentalized by the heart, or feared as a race against time.

When we turn to 'Why east wind chills', it is clear that we meet the same general attitude. Now, though, the echoing phrases 'Be content' and 'know no answer' deliver the theme more directly. I personally find this directness less rewarding than the suggestiveness of 'Should lanterns shine' where the echoes you have to be attuned to are the unstressed logical connections between sections. But 'Why east wind chills' has its own richness in the way in which it leads up to its final line 'And ghostly comets over the raised fists', which may help us see another possibility in the final 'ball' image of the other poem. 'Why east wind chills' is also a poem of echoes in a different sense from that already mentioned. The impossible questions of the first verse ('Why silk is soft and the stone wounds' etc.) are those not only of children but of wise fools in Shakespeare. These (though they have the background of serious scholastic questions in medieval and classical literature) are used because they are *impossible* questions. However, Thomas's source for such parody is John Donne, a favourite poet. In one poem Donne mocks such questions as 'Why grasse is greene, or why our blood is red'.[11] And it is from another poem by Donne that Thomas borrows the phrase that says that these answers will not be known 'till the stars go out'.[12] But more important, yet another Donne poem, 'Song' (which again parodies such questions) starts with the line 'Goe, and catche a falling starre'. That surely is the source of Thomas's 'Shall they clasp a comet in their fists?' The comet is an image for an answer impossible to catch. The image is repeated in Thomas's last line: 'And ghostly comets over the raised fists'. They are 'ghostly' because they are necessarily elusive answers. And the 'closed fists' – suggesting intellectual frustration and protest – are not what can catch them in the first place. It would be worth your considering here whether the Donne references have added anything crucial that could not have been worked out from the logic of the poem itself. And a final consideration is whether the 'ball' at the end of 'Should lanterns shine' is a parallel image for those ghostly comets.

The stance of passivity in relation to certainties and beliefs has been relatively explicit in these two poems. Looking back over the other poems we have examined in this chapter, can we claim that, implicitly, they too manifest the same attitude? They all seem, on reflection, markedly non-intellectual. Their very tone suggests the acceptance of inevitable physical process, resisting moral or philosophical emphasis in the normal sense. Description rather than prescription, one might say. The notion of being 'dumb to tell' seems generally pervasive. One even gets the impression that Thomas celebrated the worlds of organic process and bodily functions (where 'logics die') in conscious resistance to the abstract ideas which normally govern 'social' or intellectual life. Even at his most assertive and optimistic, he urges us, not towards ideas or ideologies, but towards something we might call 'vitality'. Think back to the last verse of 'When once the twilight . . .' and of 'Our eunuch dreams' and compare these final lines from other early poems:

O see the poles are kissing as they cross (p. 2)

I would be tickled by the rub that is:
Man be my metaphor (p. 12)

One sun, one manna, warmed and fed (p. 19)

. . . until, vision
Of new man strength, I seek the sun (p. 24)

We should remember the prevailing cultural and intellectual climate of Thomas's first writing decade, the 1930s. As I have already suggested, he shows a remarkable resistance to that decade's fashion for socially and politically committed poetry. Of course, his emphasis on a basically physical concept of human energy and potential may

still be related (if only in reaction) to the 1930s' sense of political
and social collapse. Thomas the man was certainly not apolitical.
His early letters show a quite radical, and argumentative, social and
political awareness. But they also, like his reviews, show a very
strong awareness of the distinction between good poetry and
propaganda.[13] It was on this ground that he forcefully criticized
poetry such as this from Stephen Spender's *Vienna* (1934):

> The live ones are
> Those who, going to work early, behold the world's
> Utter margin where all is stone and iron,
> And wrong.

Consider how different is the image of the proletariat in that second
line from the image we saw in the concluding verse of 'When once
the twilight locks no longer':

> Awake, my sleeper, to the sun,
> A worker in the morning town,
> And leave the poppied pickthank where he lies.

Yet the very image is a useful reminder of the climate in which
these strange poems were written. Again, think back to the
poem 'On no work of words' which you read at the end of
Chapter 2:

> On no work of words now for three lean months in the bloody
> Belly of the rich year and the big purse of my body
> I bitterly take to task my poverty and craft.

Isn't the basic metaphor there one of unemployment? Such traces
of the decade are interesting in a poet who seems so little concerned
to follow the political-poetical orthodoxies of his own generation.

Perhaps we should also remember that, unlike most good
poets of his generation, he was not the product of a university, which
might account for his rejection of, or indifference to, the discipline
of the intellect. This in turn might account also for the way
in which the basic moods of a non-intellectual adolescence (its
morbidity as well as its intellectual innocence) gain in his work
an unusually intuitive and prolonged expression. As you widen
your reading of the early poetry, you will be able to judge further
what qualities of insight and powers of organization are nevertheless shown there. For the time being, let me end this Chapter
by quoting one of Thomas's letters (1933). Bearing in mind
what he says here, you might afterwards read for yourself one
of the finest early poems celebrating pre-natal life – 'Before I
knocked' (p. 6).

I fail to see how the emphasising of the body can, in any way, be regarded as hideous. The body, its appearance, death, and diseases, is a fact, sure as the fact of a tree. It has its roots in the same earth as the tree. The greatest description I know of our own 'earthiness' is to be found in John Donne's Devotions, where he describes man as earth of the earth, his body earth, his hair a wild shrub growing out of the land. All thoughts and actions emanate from the body. Therefore the description of a thought or action – however abstruse it may be – can be beaten home by bringing it onto a physical level. Every idea, intuitive or intellectual, can be imaged and translated in terms of the body, its flesh, skin, blood, sinews, veins, glands, organs, cells, or senses.

Through my small, bonebound island I have learnt all I know, experienced all, and sensed all. All I write is inseparable from the island. As much as possible, therefore, I employ the scenery of the island to describe the scenery of my thoughts, the earthquakes of the body to describe the earthquakes of the heart.[14]

4. Comparisons: Some Earlier and Later Poems

In this section let us take three pairs of poems. In each pair the poems are selected from either side of a notional dividing line of 1938. In and around that year, as we saw with 'Once it was the colour of saying', Thomas seems to have been taking stock of his career to date. In comparing examples of earlier and later poems, you are likely to find the later ones more accessible in manner and matter, and you should ask yourself why this is so. I have selected poems in each pair which have broadly comparable themes, leaving us free to direct our main attention to contrasting styles (diction, imagery, tone, movement), as a way of looking back once again at some other early poems, and looking provisionally forward to the later manner.

*   *   *

Our first two poems are 'My hero bares his nerves' (p. 9) and 'In my craft or sullen art' (p. 120). They are both once again specifically about the act of writing. How would you describe the difference in sensibility and feeling between them, and what qualities in the language would you point to? The 'hero' of 'My hero bares his nerves' is the poet's inner, conscious identity, described by the body it controls and operates. We saw a similar splitting of identities in 'When once the twilight locks no longer'.

DISCUSSION

By now you will be used to the anatomical emphasis of the earlier (1933) poem. Again, the poet's inner identity (the 'hero') seems hardly distinguishable from his physical presence. In contrast, the poet of 'In my Craft or Sullen Art' (1945) seems essentially a celebrator, responding to a world of lovers, proud men, and the mighty dead – a world that lies recognizably outside himself. The tone and movement of the second poem strike one as being more relaxed and dilute. And yet on inspection it proves to be still structured by the repetition of a basic syntactic formula. Thus:

> Not for ambition or bread . . .
> But for the common wages . . .
>
> Not for the proud man apart . . .
> But for the lovers . . .

and the repetition of the poem's first line in its last once again seals in, as it were, a basically incantational music. The sense of greater relaxation, therefore, probably comes from something in the language itself. The second poem seems more orthodoxly 'romantic' or 'poetic', especially if we compare the almost anti-poetic mechanistic images of 'wire', 'box', 'chain' or 'cistern' in the earlier poem. Compare, further, these two images:

> My hero bares my side and sees his heart
> Tread, like a naked Venus,
> The beach of flesh, and wind her bloodred plait

as against

> Nor for the towering dead
> With their nightingales and psalms . . .

The second image depends surely on quite common associations being easily released from 'nightingales' and 'psalms'. The image from the earlier poem also appears to collaborate with the reader (using a simile, and inviting us perhaps to think of Botticelli's Venus). But Thomas in that first image makes a much more private leap of the imagination, seeing the heart's ascending veins and arteries as a 'bloodred plait' of hair. The earlier poem is more uncompromising, as if it didn't have the collaboration of a reading audience so positively in mind. The poet's role there is less obviously a case, to use Wordsworth's phrase, of 'a man speaking to men'. Significantly, while the poet of 'In my Craft or Sullen Art' *writes*, that of 'My hero bares his nerves' *bares*, *unpacks*, *aches*, *hugs* and *utters*. In the early poem Thomas even seems to conflate the act of writing with images suggesting masturbation. The secret sub-linguistic energies that go towards the making of a poem (the 'sharp hot stink of fox') are also celebrated in a poem by Ted Hughes – 'The Thought-Fox'.[1] You might like to compare that, too, with 'My hero bares his nerves'. It will help you to consider further to what degree Thomas sees his earlier poetry as the cool articulation (and to what degree the purgation) of private experiences. Compare, for example, the ending of Hughes's poem – 'The page is printed' – with Thomas's 'He pulls the chain, the cistern moves'.

I'd like you now to read another two poems: 'Where once the waters of your face' (1934) and 'Poem in October' (finished 1944). I think you will be struck first of all by their dissimilarity. Still, might they also have something in common with respect to theme? If so, how would you describe the different effects of style and movement that the two poems display? So please read now 'Poem in October' (p. 95) and 'Where once the waters of your face', printed below. With this earlier poem ask yourself what literal status the sea-images have. It happens that one of Thomas's local haunts as a boy was a promontory on the Gower Coast. An area near its furthest point ('Worm's Head') is alternately flooded and left dry, depending on the tide.[2] He may not have been thinking specifically of this, but it is worth allowing that there can be details, even in the early verse, that derive from things seen as well as things imagined. Yet, even so, could this early poem be called 'poetry of place' in the same way as we might use that description (Thomas actually did)[3] of 'Poem in October'?

> Where once the waters of your face
> Spun to my screws, your dry ghost blows,
> The dead turns up its eye;
> Where once the mermen through your ice
> Pushed up their hair, the dry wind steers
> Through salt and root and roe.
>
> Where once your green knots sank their splice
> Into the tided cord, there goes
> The green unraveller,
> His scissors oiled, his knife hung loose
> To cut the channels at their source
> And lay the wet fruits low.
>
> Invisible, your clocking tides
> Break on the lovebeds of the weeds;
> The weed of love's left dry;
> There round about your stones the shades
> Of children go who, from their voids,
> Cry to the dolphined sea.

Dry as a tomb, your coloured lids
Shall not be latched while magic glides
Sage on the earth and sky;
There shall be corals in your beds,
There shall be serpents in your tides,
Till all our sea-faiths die.
(p. 10)

I would say that both poems are quite clearly about the loss of some
spontaneous richness. The final lines in both cases urge a renewal
of that richness – the earlier poem through a vow ('There *shall*
be . . .') and the later poem through a prayer ('O *may* . . .'). But
this point of contact highlights even more, of course, the stylistic
differences involved, and the different relationship effected with a
literal outside world in the imagery. If the earlier poem did indeed
have a particular locale at the back of it, this now seems no longer
relevant, at least not in any detail, to our experience of reading it.
The poem clearly appropriates the world of nature reductively,
distilling it into some very privately relished images. We could not
call 'Where once the waters of your face' a *scenic* poem. The 'waters'
are literal only in as much as we could not easily find alternative
equivalents for the sea-images without completely rewriting the piece,
and losing the wider associations that naturally accompany the idea
of 'waters'. This is the sense in which, as we have seen before, the
poem has to be read 'literally'. Yet don't you also feel that the images
have a metaphoric or symbolic force, even if it is not of a kind that's
easily reduced back to any theme the images might be taken to 'stand
for'? The category of experience from which they come, or to which
they point, is not made specific. It is also not made exclusive: for
example, might not the images also suggest the human womb, in its
pre-natal and post-natal states? After all, 'waters' is the term used by
doctors for the amniotic fluid, and the second verse certainly suggests
the cutting of the umbilical cord. Then again, consider 'the waters of
your face' as a complete phrase. One thing Thomas has most certainly
done is to reverse the phrase from *Genesis* where the Holy Ghost
hovered on 'the face of the waters'. But surely this multiple
suggestiveness doesn't prevent us from feeling quite clearly that the
poem is about fruitfulness-versus-aridity. It is very much a 'Then . . .'
versus 'Now . . .' poem; and images like 'mermen', children crying
'to the dolphined sea', 'magic', 'corals', and 'sea-faiths' suggest the
loss of the child's intimate sense of wonder. This is what I feel it
shares with the later poem. But there is a major difference in the
way in which the earlier poem creates its own internal logic(s) without
relating us to the shareable outside world in the strictest sense.

In contrast, 'Poem in October' relates its theme to a literal scenic world. Its reflection of man's moods in the world of nature is obviously in a long and major tradition of English lyric poetry, bringing Wordsworth's 'Intimations of Immortality' Ode especially to mind, or the poem 'Regeneration' by Henry Vaughan. It is wonderfully alive with ordinary sights and sounds and is, amongst other things, a love poem to a particular place. Everything about it seems more confidently 'public': an evocative title which isn't (as before) simply a repetition of its first line; its memory of a 'child's/Forgotten mornings when he walked with his mother'; its atmospheric geography, and so on. And the whole movement of the verse is different. The variations of longer and shorter lines create a new sense of air and lightness. The constant run-on effect creates a more fluid, expansive movement than in earlier poems, where the basic unit seemed usually the single achieved line. One sentence in 'Poem in October' can occupy a whole stanza. Thomas himself felt pleased with its new kind of music: 'It's got, I think, a lovely slow lyrical movement'.[4]

DISCUSSION

But let us not assume that 'Poem in October' is some new kind of loose, free-wheeling verse. Look at the poem again, and consider these two questions: (a) By what means has Thomas structured his stanzas? For example, does he use rhyme? (b) What do you think is the precise distinction made between the remembered childhood of the last three verses and the adult experience of the rest of the poem?

One thing is obvious: the stanza-shape is as fixed as any we have encountered so far, but visually more interesting. Something which might surprise you, though, given the poem's fluid movement, is the fact that the number of syllables per line is consistently 9-12-9-3-5-12-12-5-3-9 in each verse. This in itself doesn't matter, but it is interesting that such meticulous counting can still produce the poem's air of freedom. Something I. A. Richards once said seems relevant here: that a poem's rhythmic effect 'is not due to our perceiving a pattern in something outside us, but to our becoming patterned ourselves'. That patterning of the reader's response comes from the rhythmic assurance of the whole poem as it develops through its descriptions and its moods. You may also have felt surprise that a poem so generally harmonious to the ear doesn't, on inspection, appear to rhyme. But in fact it does rhyme. Look at the first verse. What Thomas has used are vowel-rhymes (assonance).

Thus: *heaven . . heron . . beckon . . second . ./wood . . rook . . foot . ./shore . . wall . . forth.* Rhymes of this kind have their effect without our knowing it, linking sounds without more obviously arresting movement.

[A distinction seems to be drawn between the adult's merely appreciative sense of the picturesque (at which he might objectively 'marvel' in verse 4) and the remembered child's far more deeply-felt response, which recognized unthinkingly the indivisible oneness of man and nature (the *'true* joy of the long dead child' in the last verse). The distinction is close to that drawn by Coleridge in his 'Dejection' Ode: 'I see them all so excellently fair,/I see, not feel, how beautiful they are'. Thomas felt that childhood represented a particular way of seeing and feeling, and the precise discrimination which this suggests helps us to see 'Poem in October' as something more thoughtful than simple nostalgia.

The first example in our final pair is the opening of Thomas's most notoriously difficult poem. In 1935–36 he wrote his 'Altarwise by owl-light' sonnet sequence, and here we shall look at the first two sonnets of that sequence. The amount of commentary necessitated by all ten of the sonnets makes a discussion of the whole sequence here impossible, though the first two sonnets may lead you to explore further at a later stage.

You will find it convenient to approach the two sonnets on their own for the time being. And first of all limit yourself to two basic exercises: (a) Try to find those points where *some* aspect of the narrative seems reasonably clear; (b) Look up the following words in a dictionary: 'altarwise', 'owl-light', 'Abaddon', 'hangnail', 'mandrake', 'pelican'.

I
Altarwise by owl-light in the half-way house
The gentleman lay graveward with his furies;
Abaddon in the hangnail cracked from Adam,
And, from his fork, a dog among the fairies,
The atlas-eater with a jaw for news,   5
Bit out the mandrake with to-morrow's scream.
Then, penny-eyed, that gentleman of wounds,
Old cock from nowheres and the heaven's egg,
With bones unbuttoned to the half-way winds,
Hatched from the windy salvage on one leg,   10
Scraped at my cradle in a walking word
That night of time under the Christward shelter:
I am the long world's gentleman, he said,
And share my bed with Capricorn and Cancer.

II
Death is all metaphors, shape in one history;
The child that sucketh long is shooting up,
The planet-ducted pelican of circles
Weans on an artery the gender's strip;
Child of the short spark in a shapeless country   5
Soon sets alight a long stick from the cradle;
The horizontal cross-bones of Abaddon,
You by the cavern over the black stairs,
Rung bone and blade, the verticals of Adam,
And, manned by midnight, Jacob to the stars.   10
Hairs of your head, then said the hollow agent,
Are but the roots of nettles and of feathers
Over these groundworks thrusting through a pavement
And hemlock-headed in the wood of weathers.
(p. 65)
('Jacob' is a verb = *climb, as on Jacob's Ladder*)

After two or three readings, a new reader is probably fairly confident
of one thing: that in the first sonnet someone or something appeared
to the speaker when he was a child, and said something ('scraped
at my cradle in a walking word' l.11); and that the child-poet is
similarly addressed in the second sonnet as 'You by the cavern over
the black stairs' (l.8), with a pun on '*back*stairs'. In other words,
one probably understands that the overall narrator is the poet, who
also figures dramatically in the narrative.

Who was the visitor? Well, in the poem's own language he is
a 'gentleman of wounds, / Old cock from nowheres and the heaven's
egg, . . . / Hatched from the windy salvage on one leg'. Did you think
of Christ? He *is* Christ, who was fathered in the first place by the
Holy Ghost. He is now, however, 'hatched' again (resurrected) from
a wounding death on the upright of the cross – that 'windy salvage
on one leg'. The first sonnet's octave (last 8 lines) begins to make
at least narrative sense.

Let us consider what was said of this 'gentleman' in the sestet
(first 6 lines). Take the two opening lines:

Altarwise by owl-light in the half-way house
The gentleman lay graveward with his furies . . .

'Half-way house' might make you think of womb (between
conception and birth) or tomb (between life and a second life).
Similarly 'graveward' (in the womb, on the *way* to the grave, or
'ward' or prisoner of the grave). And again 'Altarwise': lying
horizontally, like an altar – either the foetus born to die or the corpse
actually sacrificed. In addition to womb and tomb, we might simply

think of Christ in the manger. We feel that, characteristically, one meaning doesn't drive out another. 'Owl-light' (dusk) seems appropriate to all three. 'Furies' is the remaining difficulty. But let us leave it for a moment, and try to establish the narrative of the next four lines:

> Abaddon in the hangnail cracked from Adam,
> And, from his fork, a dog among the fairies,
> The atlas-eater with a jaw for news,
> Bit out the mandrake with to-morrow's scream.

Your first difficulty here was probably syntactical, which as you now know is a characteristic problem with the poetry. 'Cracked (from)' is a main verb, not a past-participle. (If you look closely you'll see that it *can* only be a main verb.) Its subject is Abaddon (= Angel of Death). With Adam it would be useful to remember that Christ was called the second Adam, but even thinking of the first Adam would not lead you astray. At some event, then, Death (Abaddon) split away from Man (Adam/Christ). This would suitably describe the significance of the conception, birth, and death of Christ, singly or all three. But some prominence is given the crucifixion by that word 'hangnail'. Literally a piece of skin hanging loose from near a finger-nail, its two component words – *hang* and *nail* – suggest the cross. Then Thomas uses the image of the crucifixion as a castration, with God (the 'atlas-eater', world-devourer) biting out the sexual, death-producing aspects of man in the suffering Christ, like a dog uprooting the 'mandrake' plant in the old legend. The original mandrake, on being uprooted, uttered a scream that could kill. That was why a dog was used to uproot it. And that in turn is why the 'atlas-eater' here is a 'dog among the fairies' (suggesting also God among lesser gods). He has a 'jaw for news' (cf. *a nose for news*) because 'the mandrake with to-morrow's scream' is the penis, capable of creating tomorrow's progeny. The 'furies' in the second line are therefore probably the sexual appetites that died with the mortal body of Christ. It is the *im*mortal Christ who appears to the child in his cradle, and speaks to him the substance of the second sonnet. It is possible that the child thus visited is not only the poet but the Christ-child Himself. With time collapsed in this way, the manger would be both 'the Christward shelter' and 'the cavern over the black stairs', evoking the resurrected Christ's harrowing of hell.

I don't propose to paraphrase the second sonnet in the same detail. Much of its meaning will in any case spring from the commentary above. This seems, however, a good stage at which to remind you

of a point I have tended to emphasize in a preliminary way earlier
in this study. And that is, what we mean when we say that Thomas's
poetry should be read 'literally'. With reference to these sonnets, you
will certainly have felt that the events don't belong to any 'literal'
world in the ordinary sense. 'Literal' was, rather, the word Thomas
tended to use of the sort of *reading* his poetry demanded. And he
made the point strongly in disagreement with Edith Sitwell's
interpretation of the lines

> The atlas-eater with a jaw for news,
> Bit out the mandrake with to-morrow's scream.

She had said that the lines described 'the violent speed and the
sensation-loving, horror-loving craze of modern life'. Thomas replied
'She doesn't take the literal meaning: that a world-devouring ghost
creature bit out the horror of tomorrow from a gentleman's loins'.[5]
Where Edith Sitwell strikes us as being simply wrong, Thomas's
comment may seem simply unhelpful, giving the lines over again in
their own terms. But that's exactly the point. Edith Sitwell's error
was to imagine that there was some much vaguer general theme
which was simply 'represented' in these particular images. Of course,
we too have to some degree used a preconception of the 'theme' to
set the images into some kind of logical relationship. And indeed,
an understanding of language, of any kind, demands that we do so.
But Edith Sitwell went one step further. She got what she thought
to be the theme, and then discarded the images. Much more
important than 'theme' for Thomas is narrative. And he writes in
the early poems in such a way as to retain us within that narrative.
This is what makes Thomas essentially a Modernist poet: he forces
us to draw our meanings from the logic of the poem itself, in concrete
terms, and not from an appeal to general experience outside the
verbal event of the poem. This is the sense in which so much
Modernist verse, though in a variety of ways, is irreducible. (For
a fuller discussion of Thomas's Modernism, see below, pp. 106–115.)
The most important thing that one can offer with Thomas's earlier
poetry is some guidance as to the narrative.

I'd like you now to re-read the two sonnets, surrendering to
their narrative as an actual event taking place on (and in) its own
terms, and not as a replacement-allegory standing for something
else. Even the 'Christian' context of the images can be appealed
to only up to a certain point, because the very tone of the images
shows that the Christian materials are not being used in any
traditional way.

Now look at a later poem, written in 1945. It is titled 'The
Conversation of Prayer'.

The conversation of prayers about to be said
By the child going to bed and the man on the stairs
Who climbs to his dying love in her high room.
The one not caring to whom in his sleep he will move
And the other full of tears that she will be dead,

Turns in the dark on the sound they know will arise
Into the answering skies from the green ground,
From the man on the stairs and the child by his bed.
The sound about to be said in the two prayers
For the sleep in a safe land and the love who dies

Will be the same grief flying. Whom shall they calm?
Shall the child sleep unharmed or the man be crying?
The conversation of prayers about to be said
Turns on the quick and the dead, and the man on the stairs
To-night shall find no dying but alive and warm

In the fire of his care his love in the high room.
And the child not caring to whom he climbs his prayer
Shall drown in a grief as deep as his true grave,
And mark the dark eyed wave, through the eyes of sleep,
Dragging him up the stairs to one who lies dead.
(p. 93)

I don't think I am contradicting what I said above when I say
that it is an interest in a common theme that prompts me to
juxtapose the two sonnets and 'The Conversation of Prayer'. In
fact, it may reinforce my point. What I think they have in common
is not any comparable details as such but the dramatization of
the meeting-point between innocence and experience. And this is
not so much a 'theme' as a dramatic device. The crucified Christ
addressing the newly-born child; a young boy experiencing by
some mysterious exchange the tragic nightmare of the adult:
already any common ground between the two will appear to you
notional, or simply convenient. The two poems are so differently
conceived, and involve such different narratives. But even that
notional comparison may be helpful in drawing the poems together
for a contrast of their styles. And what I'd like you to do now is
select some details to illustrate the difference between 'The
Conversation of Prayer' and the sonnets in terms of imagery, texture,
and verse-movement. These aspects of 'The Conversation of Prayer'
should again be responded to only within the 'literal' assertions of
the narrative.

Here are some points to compare with your own. Obviously, we get a strong sense of the *ordinary* in the later poem, despite the mysterious exchange of answers given to the two prayers. We are struck not only by ordinary references such as 'the child going to bed' or 'the man on the stairs', but by the ordinariness also of cliché, as in 'full of tears' or 'the quick and the dead'. In contrast, we might almost have characterized the earlier style by saying it was a studied *avoidance* of cliché: indeed, a case of never calling a spade a spade, if Thomas could help it – even allowing that the actual spade exists outside the poem! In the second sonnet, for example, 'the child that sucketh long' is not long a child: it soon becomes 'the gender's strip', weaned 'on an artery', and 'a long stick from the cradle'. The self-sacrificing mother, whose blood and milk feed the child, is similarly 'The planet-ducted pelican of circles' etc.

With such indirect identities, we tend in the earlier poem, and the earlier poetry generally, to be aware of concrete parts (bone, blade, hairs) as opposed to conceptual wholes in the later (child, man, his 'love in her high room'). In this way, the earlier texture is much starker, even though some local intensities like 'the dark eyed wave' in the later poem here sometimes remind us of the earlier voice. The general perspective seems radically different. The language of an earlier poem embroils us in its physical sensations. The language of 'The Conversation of Prayer' on the other hand seems to stand over against the experience, instead of *becoming* the experience in itself. This greater sense of leisure is evident also in the way in which the idea of foreshortened time (of death instantaneously perceived in life) is presented. In the 'Altarwise' sonnets, a single image will give it:

> Hairs of your head, then said the hollow agent,
> Are but the roots of nettles and of feathers.

In the later poem, the exchanged prayers of the child and the man slowly develop into an extended image which structures the *whole* poem. And a reflection of the whole is there in the pun on 'conversation': it is also the *conversion* of prayers.

Tying in with these points is the different movement of the verse. Once again in the earlier example the basic unit seems to be the individual line, individually relished and weighted. 'The Conversation of Prayer' has a slow, self-echoing movement which seems to bind the whole into a consistent music. Notice, for example, that only the last of its verses is end-stopped. And notice the rhyme-scheme. End-words constantly rhyme inwards with words in the middle of the lines, again making us think of the whole rather than of individual achieved lines.

These six examples illustrate something of the range in Thomas from 'obscure' to 'relatively straightforward'. And no doubt you found the later poem in each pair the easier to read and grasp. But I think we should ask again, more pointedly, what we mean when we say an early poem is difficult. And do we mean that the later ones are not? In bringing up more general questions in this respect, I am not expecting them to be answered straightforwardly at this stage. Your own answers will be formulated gradually in a wider reading of the poems, when I would ask you to bear some of the following points in mind.

For example, does an early poem *remain* difficult when the reader has, perhaps convincingly, been taken through it with guidance from a critical commentary? The important test here, of course, is whether the meanings you have 'worked out', often strenuously, can be retained *spontaneously* when you return to read the poem as a whole. That is, are they summoned up authoritatively and cohesively by the poem itself? A poem which comes to life only next door, as it were, to a critical commentary can hardly be called meaningful in a real sense. In my own experience, very few of Thomas's poems fail to meet this test. Examples of what I would personally consider failures in this respect are 'Now' (p. 46), 'A grief ago' (p. 49) and 'How soon the servant sun' (p. 51). But you should make a point of testing my view against your own reading of these poems. Having read them independently first of all, consider them further in the light of the detailed commentaries by W. Y. Tindall in his *A Reader's Guide to Dylan Thomas* (see 'Further Reading' below, p. 131). Then, on returning to the poems, ask yourself if the aspects of Tindall's commentary that you found persuasive can be retained spontaneously when you return to re-reading the poems on their own. Do the poems themselves allow us natural points of access into the overall *logic* that brings the images into relationship?

Consider the question of obscurity from another angle. When syntax, narrative, and so on have been worked out in an early poem, does any problem remain as to Thomas's attitude or tone? Are the latter in any way obscure or ambiguous *in themselves*? After all, attitude and tone can remain richly problematic in poems considered much less difficult than Thomas's at first reading. For instance, Yeats's 'Sailing to Byzantium'. Ostensibly, that poem urges the ideal superiority of art over organic physical life. But Yeats's attitude to both remains complex, ambiguous – as, on the same theme, does Keats's attitude in 'Ode on a Grecian Urn'. We've seen Thomas's early tendency to conflate images from different categories of experience, but not (I would have thought) in ways that bring irony, or ambiguity of attitudes, or difficult ideas into play. On the whole, in the earlier poem, I think we know simply and directly where Thomas stands, once we've decided what the syntax and the narrative say.

The two 'Altarwise' sonnets may be an exception. One is puzzled as to what use exactly the Christian story is being put. Puzzled, too, by the coexistence of a cocky, sacrilegious note with lines of resounding gravity. Is the Christian story being used dramatically only, and not as a matter of actual belief? If you decide to tackle the whole sequence, I think you will find that finally *this* is the difficult question – more, even, than the obscurity of syntax or image along the way.

But the same problem, though in much simpler form, may be posed by the later poem, 'The Conversation of Prayer'. Not a problem of tone and attitude. I think one is much surer of tone here than in the 'Altarwise' sonnets: a humane, sympathetic one. But ask yourself what questions concerning Thomas's actual *beliefs* might come to mind when we read 'The Conversation of Prayer'. And are they relevant?

For example, in 'The Conversation of Prayer' is Thomas implying that human prayers are not heard at all; or heard and arbitrarily ignored; or are they heard and ignored for a reason – so that each individual has to experience suffering in the growth to maturity; or are they heard and answered kindly only for those (like the man in the poem) whose concern is selflessly for another human being? Personally, I feel the poem does not centre on this question of belief at all, but on the inevitability of suffering and disillusion (foretasted by the child in his unaccountable nightmare). I think the child is Thomas's real concern. The man, and the religious implications of 'prayer', I feel are ways of dramatizing this meeting-ground between innocence and experience. As in the 'Altarwise' sonnets, I think Thomas is employing religion as a pattern (generally familiar) within which to work. This is not, however, to agree with the view of a critic such as John Wain, that Thomas is only conveniently 'thumbing a lift' from religion:

> religion . . . seems to me Thomas's worst pitch; he never succeeds in making me feel that he is doing more than thumbing a lift from it. Indeed it is only a helpful subject to him in those poems which are content to leave every important matter to be settled by the reader: the line 'After the first death, there is no other' has been praised as an example of significant ambiguity (either 'when you are dead there's an end of it' or 'after this mortal life comes the eternal one'), and no doubt that is very valuable, but if a poet is going to be a religious poet there has (one would think) to be a little more definition about it.[6]

There are always, surely, received patterns of thought (myths and images) within a culture, on which one draws, not necessarily in strict belief, but in order to make thought itself possible in the first place. The line 'After the first death, there is no other' which Wain quotes is from 'A Refusal to Mourn the Death, by Fire, of a Child in London'. We shall raise the question of its 'ambiguity' in the next chapter.

But one thing seems likely. The more dilute and 'open' Thomas's later style becomes, the more nakedly will this question of his actual beliefs, or the general question of his 'ideas' or feelings, appear. The textural difficulty of an earlier poem deflects attention from the nature of its thought or implications, or at least delays attention to these things. In the end what an early poem adds up to is a concrete narrative, not a conceptual statement with which we might agree or disagree, or which we might find adequate or inadequate. In this way, paradoxically, it is perhaps the later poems which run the greater risks. You might like to test this further in an exercise you can do independently. David Aivaz described 'Incarnate devil' (1955, p. 35). and 'This Side of the Truth' (1945, p. 98) as the only poems by Thomas in which 'morality is a theme'.[7] There is some validity in this, if what we mean is that these two poems challenge, with uncharacteristic pointedness, the choice man is traditionally enjoined to make between Good and Evil. The earlier poem implies, and the later poem affirms, that notions of Good and Evil are man's invention, superimposed on a morally neutral, though dynamic, universe. However, the difference between implying and affirming is crucial, and brings up again the contrasts of style (evoked via comparisons of themes) that this chapter has sought to illustrate. As David Aivaz says, 'This Side of the Truth' is 'as bare of imagery and as close to public statement as a poem by Thomas can be'. So with that poem you are likely to find yourself more prompted, certainly than has generally been the case so far, to judge the validity of what is actually being said. As it happens, Aivaz claims that the poem introduces a moral perspective even while rejecting it:

> Despite the elegiac tone and tread, I suspect that [Thomas] is here defining a position in order to have done with it. Still, he has not wholly committed himself. The title of the poem is 'This Side of the Truth'; and to write of 'the innoce dark, and the guilty dark', the 'good death, and bad death', is ne beat on 'dark' and 'death' notwithstanding, in some way to d .guish them. There is some evidence in Thomas's later poems that his world is developing. The development . . . may be for him the other side of the truth of process and intrinsically moral: the greater its extent, the 'better'. It remains true, however, that the chief theme of Biblical imagery is one of celebration, and not of choice.

Nevertheless, the poem claims that Good and Bad (or their physical manifestations) disappear ultimately into non-judgement. What is your opinion of the fact that Thomas calls this 'unjudging love'? 'Incarnate devil' contains very different materials but seems to be written from the same point of view. Try to judge the difference its style makes to that point of view, and to your reaction to it. As an entry into that earlier poem, you might take the following description by Clark Emery:

> I think that Thomas, like Blake, is of the Devil's party. It is sex, of course, that in the shaping-time of adolescence destroys the innocence of childhood. But it is not a devil but a bearded, Thou-Shalt-Notting Jehovah (invented by the tabu-makers) who, speaking with forked tongue, enunciated the false distinction ('cloven myth'): namely, that sexuality is hell and asceticism (an extinguishing of warmth and light) is heaven. And then, himself to blame for destroying the possibility of innocence in sexuality, is given credit for saving the remorseful sinner from the clutches of the Devil. There is in the poem no devil at all. There is only the Jehovah-image which, from Thomas's point of view, is devilish.[8]

5. Thomas and Friends

The poems on poetry which we looked at in Chapter 2 came from Thomas's third collection, *The Map of Love* (1939). Their presence there, along with others querying the nature of his own earlier verse, helps us see *The Map of Love* as a transitional volume. Also remarkable in that volume is the number of poems which, for the first time, respond to the independent reality of other people. These presumably illustrate in practice what Thomas advertised in principle in 'Once it was the colour of saying', namely his need to break out of a kind of personal deadlock of theme and range, as well as of style. Naturally, poems involving outside events, other people, and human relationships, would present a particular challenge in this respect. And the poetry does indeed widen to include love poems, the birth of his first child on the eve of wartime, the events of war itself, and other occasional subjects. But I feel sure that, if you have already found these strangely missing in the verse you've encountered so far, you will also imagine that, when they begin to come into Thomas's range, he will make something still highly personal and characteristic out of them. I should like you therefore, in this section, to look at some quite different poems which respond to the lives and deaths of other people.

* * *

Let's return to 1938 to take our first example – 'After the funeral (In memory of Ann Jones)'. Ann Jones was the poet's aunt at whose farm, Fernhill, Thomas had spent some of the happiest periods of his childhood. I'd like you to read the poem now (p. 80). After one or two readings you might, (a) first of all work out the syntax of the first 15 lines, and ask yourself what time-sequence is involved in those lines. Is everything in its strict order? What kind of effect is produced by those lines? And (b) prepare to think ultimately of the poem's strengths and interest as a poem of relationship. What is Thomas's attitude to Ann Jones? Is it complicated in any way? Is it an attitude to more than just a person? Is the nature of her religion also in question? Think particularly of the images associated with Ann Jones from line 13 onwards. (c) What role does Nature play in the poem's treatment of its theme? (d) We've seen that Thomas's poems are often self-consciously concerned with his own role as poet. Is this also reflected in 'After the funeral? In what ways? Does this strike you as inappropriate in an elegy? And (e) how would you describe the poem's style and movement?

DISCUSSION

(a) The opening lines have a density and concreteness we probably associate more with the earlier than with the later verse, with close physical images taking precedence over any more leisurely statement. In considering the syntax of the first 11 lines, did you notice that it is governed by that one opening word 'After . . .', and that the main verb ('I stand') is delayed until line 12? This postpones not only our grasp of syntax, but our understanding of the time-sequence involved. Presumably the actual sequence was as follows. 'Morning smack' of the gravedigger's spade (l. 6), opening the grave, woke up the young boy on the morning of the funeral. Then the actual burial service (ll. 1–5) where the mourners are described. Then the 'feast' (l. 10) – if literal, possibly the usual meal for the visiting mourners. Then Thomas standing alone in the room, 'for this memorial's sake' (that is, for the sake of writing this poem). Ann's body isn't actually there, but present nevertheless to Thomas's imagination. When was this? Immediately after everyone else had gone? Most probably. But possibly also on a later visit.

I think this delay and indirection are important to the effect Thomas wants to create. The lines seem to me suitably claustro-phobic and oppressive. The line about the 'desolate boy' slitting his throat in the dark of the coffin and shedding 'dry leaves' is of course metaphorical. It suggests a nightmare of despair between sleep and waking, but seems also to gather into itself the claustrophobia of the occasion. The oddly arranged impressions also seem true to the way in which emotional crises or mixed feelings often impressionistically jumble our sensations. Whether immediately after the event or later, it is from this trauma of an artificial occasion that Thomas wants to free himself in writing the poem. That trauma had produced (to his view) a hypocritical grief in others, and not enough real grief in himself. Against this resistant opening (resistant to us in the reading as it was to him in the event), he wants to make Ann's virtues survive the event and 'occasion' of her death.

(b) Thomas speaks of 'her love' (l. 25), and one gets an overall impression of profound respect and affection for the dead woman. But we are surely also made to feel that her personality was tied in with her puritanical religion and her stultified domestic setting. The image of her hands lying 'with religion in their cramp' (l. 32) refers of course to Ann Jones in death. But it was led up to by other mysteriously ambiguous touches like her '*hooded*, fountain heart', her '*wood*-tongued virtue' or her '*bent* spirit'. And the images of halted life, made powerfully central to the whole poem – the 'stuffed fox' and 'stale fern' – were after all very much her own emblems. This complicated response seems to me one of the great things about the poem. Thomas is responding fully, not only to a remembered individual, but to a particular religious culture and a way of life, which were for him inadequate reflections of Ann's real love and kindness. The grotesque satire of the mourners in the opening lines, however, modulates into a more searching ambiguity where Ann Jones as an individual is concerned.

(c) Against all the human, domestic, and religious inadequacies stands the context of Nature. Look at lines 21–26. Remembering the earlier poems, what seems to you new about those lines? They contain what I can only call an appeal to Nature, seen as a new, affirmative context. The fern and the fox are alive there – 'the ferned and foxy woods' – a nice touch that. It seems very different from the 'elemental' Nature of the earlier poems, more spontaneous and sacramental, as if now tied in with a sense of values. Thomas finds a new kind of norm there. It hasn't yet reached the open descriptiveness we saw in 'Poem in October', and which we shall see again in other later poems in our next chapter, but it already seems potent.

(d) Another important aspect is Thomas's consciousness of himself as celebrating artist. There is a sense in which the poem is also about itself, as lines 36–7 indicate – 'this monumental/Argument of the hewn voice' (which I hope reminds you of the poem-as-stone image of 'The spire cranes'). And 'How shall my animal' may also return to mind: Thomas is aware that Ann's virtue may not come through livingly enough in the different reality of words. The memorial might prove merely marmorial. Hence the 'skyward statue (l. 27) as an image also for the poem itself, 'carved from' the reality, and possibly as dead as the corpse's 'seventy years of stone'. It is now also feasible to see the 'dry leaves' of line 8 not only as the absence of tears but as the 'dry leaves' of an abortive earlier poem. (Thomas did in fact write an arid poem at the time of Ann's actual death in 1933: the present poem was written five years later).[1]

We shall return later to this self-reflexive tendency as a specific aspect of Modernist poetry. Did you find the self-conscious concern with himself as poet a breach of tact in this particular case? I would personally argue otherwise. For all that the poem may be a colossal carved thing in words, Thomas seems to feel that this is his only medium for praise now that Ann Jones is dead. And, after all, what he shows is essentially self-criticism of the large gestures of his own style, though without abandoning his role as celebrator. He understands that an elegy *has* to make a conscious bid for survival, must loom large, even if vulnerably so. The choice was between making the poem a discreet epitaph and making it mime a resurrection, by swelling his protest and celebration until the very emblems of tamed and halted life revive; until

The stuffed lung of the fox twitch and cry Love
And the strutting fern lay seeds on the black sill.

Fear concerning the inertness of language seems appropriate in a poem that fears also the inertness of custom, ceremony, and of death itself.

(e) The poem is chronologically the first where I sense, taking its overall effect, a basically new style: expansive and accumulative in tone, emotion, and movement. Later poems tend to develop these qualities while also structuring them (as 'After the funeral' does not) in a variety of large stanza-forms. The structuring or control in 'After the funeral' comes in a different way: the last fourteen lines of the poem reveal a more deliberate economy of articulation. It is as if, in view of the larger gestures of his craft, Thomas had taken special pains to make individual lines strike home with a hard clarity of perception: lines such as 'Her fist of a face died clenched on a round pain' or 'And the strutting fern lay seeds on the black sill'. Remembering that the poem shares its date (1938) with 'Once it was the colour of saying', we might say that such lines are good examples of the aim of winding every stone off like a reel. Not in the sense of verbal austerity alone – indeed, the later poems are on the whole verbally more, not less, expansive. There was also the aim of choosing morally more demanding subjects. And the subjects that applied that kind of resistant challenge in Thomas's case were subjects that demanded attention to outside realities. 'After the funeral' is an example of how those realities also include human relationships. The biographical actuality of a real person like Ann Jones did not become a characteristic feature of his verse. But by momentarily pointing in that potential direction, 'After the funeral' has the status of a transitional poem in theme as well as style. Interestingly, Thomas placed the poem between 'The spire cranes' and 'Once it was the colour of saying' in the 1939 collection.

In any case, poems of relationship do not necessarily have to be about real people. In this connection, it is worth our looking at another poem from 1938. The fact that, like 'After the funeral', it involved the transformation of an earlier attempt of 1933 reinforces its 'transitional' nature. Like 'After the funeral', it shows that the failure of the poetry of human relationship in 1933 could be redeemed through a new kind of effort in 1938.[2] The poem is 'The tombstone told when she died' (p. 86). You might again start by working out the time-sequence involved. Does this seem to you just wilfully obscure? What experience exactly is suggested by the woman's own words in the last five lines? With these questions in mind, please read the poem now.

DISCUSSION

Thomas described it as a 'Hardy-like' poem,[3] presumably because of the anecdotal oddity evoked by the woman's two surnames on the tombstone. But the indirection of what follows the matter-of-factness of the first three lines is anything but 'Hardy-like'. The time-sequence, in terms of mere chronology, is simple enough. The woman died before the poet was conceived; however, her experience was later communicated to the poet when he lay unborn in his mother's womb; as a grown man he comes across the grave 'by luck' and, as if in her words, is told more specifically what happened; later, other men tell him the story. But, though clear, these different stages seem to merge. The arrangement might even be accused of being merely untidy and needlessly misleading. For example,

> She married in this pouring place,
> That I struck one day by luck
> Before I heard in my mother's side . . .

That third line tells when 'she married', not when he 'struck' upon the place – but we momentarily hear the other possibility. (Test how the line 'Among men later I heard it said' has a similar misleading effect in the third verse.) But tidy directness of that kind isn't aimed for. There is however a new directness in the simplicity of the language itself. This contrasts with the mysterious mixing and merging of times and experiences, but also helps the poem gain exactly that effect. Thus the 'mortal wall' of the womb parallels the 'thick stone' on the grave in a way that contrasts respectively what the one can and the other cannot 'tell' of the tragedy. Again, we sense a connection between 'plunged':

> With a hand plunged through her hair

and 'floods':

> And the dear floods of his hair.

But most important of all is the very poignancy of the harsh tragedy being witnessed by the unborn child. The sensitivity of that witness is suggested by the different connotations of 'the room of a secret child' as against gossip later 'among men'. And that sensitive inwardness is what leads to the poignant ambiguity of what is referred to in the woman's imagined words at the end. She died in a fit of insanity ('this mad heroine') before the bridal night. 'Among men', the story is retailed as simply a mad fear of sexuality. And violent sexual penetration is indeed imaged in her own words at the end. But those same words are surely measured in such a way as to suggest also the birth of a boy child:

> I died before bedtime came
> But my womb was bellowing
> And I felt with my bare fall
> A blazing red harsh head tear up
> And the dear floods of his hair.

The 'dear floods' are also those of the wet, matted hair of the newly born. Conception and actual birth are merged in a way that matches the wider mysteriousness of the whole poem. Significantly, Thomas thought that the word 'dear' in that last line was 'daring': 'I wanted the girl's *terrible* reaction to orgiastic [orgasmic] death to be suddenly altered into a kind of despairing love. As I see it now, it strikes me as very moving'.[4]

The next poem involves again the death of someone not personally known to Thomas, a girl killed in the wartime bombing in London. The Second World War had a profound effect on Thomas the man. He felt a sense of deep moral shock and outrage, a response not usually associated with the Bohemian legend surrounding him. But the poems this produced are at some remove from raw feelings. He somehow saw it as his duty and impulse to respond affirmatively rather than negatively to this, the only historic event to gain entry into his often intensely private poetic world. That affirmative quality is caught even in the titles of the poems written on the events of war: 'Deaths *and* Entrances' (1940), '*Ceremony* After a Fire Raid' (1944), 'A *Refusal* to Mourn the Death, by Fire, of a Child in London' (1945). That last is the poem we shall consider here. Please read 'A Refusal to Mourn' (p. 94) now. Ask yourself what function it seems to set itself as an elegy. In particular, in what sense is it a *refusal* to mourn? Leading on from that, and bearing in mind that some kind of 'consolation' is appropriate to an elegy, what sort of consolation is offered here? And what precise meaning do you get from the poem's final line?

DISCUSSION

A few points about style first of all. If we hyphenate and punctuate the following words in the opening lines we can see that they form a series of compound adjectives describing 'darkness': 'mankind-making', 'Bird-beast-and-flower-Fathering', 'and all-humbling' (darkness). By omitting the hyphens and commas, Thomas creates (without comment) the impression of unity and one-ness that governs his approach to the tragedy. (Also relevant to his theme is the fact that *Birds, Beasts and Flowers* was the title of one of D. H. Lawrence's volumes of poetry – a volume celebrating the intensity and integrity of non-human organic life.) But though the style aims at an accumulative and wheeling general effect, one aspect is very different from what we saw in the early poetry. You will remember that there I used the word periphrasis for Thomas's tendency to delight in describing things in a round-about way. The subject-matter of his poetry became an 'animal' in 'How shall my animal' – and the 'animal' idea then took over! More traditionally periphrastic are some of the images in this present poem. Take 'sow my salt seed' in the second verse. Its idea is that of dropping a tear. The word 'salt' keeps us in touch with the real referent while at the same time 'sow' and 'seed' suggest a momentary comparison with something else. It isn't a complete metaphor because the substitution of one thing for another is not complete, and equally important is the element of ritual circumlocution that such phrases represent. (Our previous analogy – p. 20 above – was the phrase 'finny tribe' for fish.) I feel that the same element is there in 'the round/Zion of the water bead', 'the synagogue of the ear of corn', 'the stations of the breath' and 'the long friends'. Of course, the metaphoric life in these phrases is immeasurably more real and exciting than anything that could come from calling fish 'the finny tribe' or barley 'the bearded product'. The 'long friends' for example evokes, all at once, people long since dead and the roots and worms in the earth under the man-made, and now man-burnt, city. But in none of these phrases is the metaphor pursued. Each separate circumlocution adds, however, to our impression of the poet's priestly concept of his role.

This brings us to the more general questions I asked above about the kind of elegy the poem represents. In one sense, of course, the poem does what its title says it refuses to do. For example, the poem doesn't refuse to be moved by, or to move us with, the event. But it does refuse to mourn in the sense in which one might make political or doctrinal or sentimental capital out of the death. (I feel those three possibilities are pointed to in the third verse.) The broader perspective offered by the first two stanzas is also relevant here. What Thomas really does is not refuse to mourn, but postpone the mourning, 'until' . . . Until when? Until all things (animal, vegetable, and human) return to their first origins in that primal darkness which made, fathered, and humbled all. But that darkness isn't felt to be a void. Consider the sacramental nature of the images in the second verse. And consider the ambiguity with which things are said to have an end: the darkness *tells* with silence; the last light is described as *breaking*; the still hour has the sea *tumbling* in harness. The postponement of mourning is in effect its cancellation. There will come a time when mourning will cease to be a relevant possibility, when the gap between natural organic process and human social interpretation or emotion is finally closed. And it is against that long perspective, the poem seems to say, that man's tendency to describe and label and mourn a tragedy is to be seen. This resistance to immediate answers, immediate convictions, should perhaps remind us of the theme of 'Should lanterns shine' and 'Why east wind chills' (see pp. 42–45 above).

This is also a good point at which to raise again the question touched on at the end of the last chapter: about how much more nakedly we confront Thomas's 'ideas' in the later poems. No doubt an important part of your experience of reading this particular poem was your own feeling about the moral rightness of what is said, or about its adequacy to the event. The poem has a brave assertiveness. It braves the possible charges of callousness, or inadequacy, or simplification, rather as does W. B. Yeats's stance of 'tragic gaiety' in his late poems. You may even feel that it does not so much brave these charges as flout them. Either way, this is the area in which you will no doubt test the poem's value. It has at least to be faced up to, that Thomas is sticking to the only religious perspective that seems to him true: a kind of celebratory pantheism. At death, man becomes part of an organic, unmourning universe. Therefore, however many meanings may appear to crowd into the poem's last line –

>   After the first death, there is no other

– only one is totally sanctioned by the whole elegy: neither a Christian resurrection nor a total nothingness; something beyond either victory or defeat. But we should at least note the possibility of a specific Biblical allusion. At several points (e.g. xxi, 8) the Book of *Revelation* speaks of the 'second death' (= eternal death) that will come upon the ungodly at the Day of Judgement. There is ample evidence in the poetry as a whole that such Biblical allusions in Thomas are not accidental. Nor would the allusion here be gratuitous or only vaguely ambiguous: the poet would be specifically denying the survival of what we normally call conscious life, capable of further judgement and a 'second death'. The way in which we finally take the line (however pregnant its meanings may be) is surely dictated by the tenor of the whole poem. Again, if 'the first death' refers to something more than just this girl's death, we are still in a position to gauge from where exactly it derives its main meaning. Thus if we feel that it could allude to Christ's death (the first death to be overcome by resurrection) we would have to ask, surely, whether that degree of orthodox belief follows naturally from the more purely organic emphasis of the poem as a whole. We should certainly notice that 'the first death' echoes 'the first dead'. The point seems to be that all those who have died before have physically given human significance to the organic cycle which the girl now re-enters. This is the central strain in Thomas as a religious poet, and you might like now to consider such poems as 'And death shall have no dominion' (1933, p. 62) or 'When all my five and country senses see' (1938, p. 74) in this connection. It may already have occurred to you that we haven't travelled all that far, in terms of essential ideas, from 'Light breaks where no sun shines' – 'Above the waste allotments the dawn halts' (see above, pp. 32–33).

But having said that, let us see whether Thomas was capable also of responding to the events of war in a more orthodoxly moral way. In suggesting this difference in our next poem, we should however be prepared by now to find the orthodox still expressed in unorthodox ways. Please now read 'There was a Saviour' (p. 117). Ask yourself what images evoke the poem's attitude to the 'Saviour' in the first three verses, and through what stages that attitude develops. Which images establish the context of war? Consider your own response against the interpretation that follows.

DISCUSSION

Christ is evoked in his mystery ('rarer than radium'), his mysterious ordinariness ('Commoner than water'), and in the radical challenge of his teaching ('crueller than truth'). But that challenge seems at once to be described as having been misinterpreted and misused. 'Children kept from the sun' suggests both those adults who childishly simplified His teaching and (a nice suggestion) the literal children of Sunday Schools down the centuries. In both cases, their ability to see moral problems has been replaced by a process that has turned the Saviour's message of open love ('keyless smiles') into the 'jails' and 'studies' of organized religion. The teaching's real message called for uncomfortable commitment ('unrest', 'murdering breath', 'the tremendous shout', 'tears'). But man has made of it, instead, the comfortable or unreal retreat suggested by words such as 'locked', 'calm', 'safe', 'hid', 'silence', 'liars', 'asylums' and 'churches'. Instead of individually responsible grief (crying 'On to the ground when a man died') our tears are put 'for joy in the unearthly flood' of metaphysical belief; we listen for response only from the 'cloud-formed shell' of heaven. Then in the last line of the third verse a new situation is evoked –

Now in the dark there is only yourself and myself.

It suggests first of all a society in which comforting religious belief has in any case disappeared. But the specific situation of war is what is developed in the final two verses. The 'dark' becomes the black-out of that war, in which the speaker and another modern representative of complacent religion are two 'blacked brothers' who find this year of the war (the poem was written in early 1940) 'hollow and inhospitable' to their cry of despair. Notice how their failure of ordinary sympathy before this actual war now suggests the very events which led up to that conflict, forecasting 'Greed on man beating near and fire neighbour'. And the new moral sympathy for others that the war precipitates is evoked in a startling way. The demolished cities yield a terrifyingly literal image for the reality of other people's lives. The 'dust' of 'strangers' is seen literally to

Ride through the doors of our unentered house.

And it is this that arouses a new love. In as much as it is both 'silk and rough', that love reminds us of Christ's. It breaks the 'rock' of privacy and cruelty. But the rock that it breaks may also, finally, be the rock on which Christ built his church. (An added irony here is that the poem was consciously written in the stanza-form of Milton's 'On the Morning of Christ's Nativity'.) The poem remains ambiguous on the supernatural validity of Christianity itself, but its insistence on the theme of ordinary sympathy usefully supplements the pantheistic consolation of 'A Refusal to Mourn'. You should decide for yourself the degree to which the ornateness of language and image still pulls away from the directness of such a theme. You might consider this point in relation to another war-elegy, 'Among those Killed in the Dawn Raid was a Man Aged a Hundred' (p. 127). The title suggests (and was) a verbatim transcription from a newspaper headline. As such, its point was ironical: the technology of war employed to kill a man already near death! And the irony is still alive in the opening lines: 'The locks [of his bodily frame] yawned loose and a blast blew them wide'. But in reading the poem you might consider how long a tone of irony, demanding under-statement, can survive in any Thomas poem.

I'd like you now to consider a poem Thomas wrote and addressed to his father, as the latter faced the double darkness of blindness and death. He had always profoundly respected his father, though standing in some awe of his severity, strength of character, and independent judgement. These are the qualities which Thomas sees as being tamed in illness. The poem is 'Do not go gentle into that good night'. Thomas completed it in July 1951. You probably won't find it particularly difficult, and on reading it through once or twice you should try to describe for yourself its general emotive force. It is a poem of considerable technical interest, however, so perhaps we can approach it first from that point of view after you've read it. Here it is:

> Do not go gentle into that good night,
> Old age should burn and rave at close of day;
> Rage, rage against the dying of the light.
>
> Though wise men at their end know dark is right,
> Because their words had forked no lightning they
> Do not go gentle into that good night.
>
> Good men, the last wave by, crying how bright
> Their frail deeds might have danced in a green bay,
> Rage, rage against the dying of the light.
>
> Wild men who caught and sang the sun in flight,
> And learn, too late, they grieved it on its way,
> Do not go gentle into that good night.
>
> Grave men, near death, who see with blinding sight
> Blind eyes could blaze like meteors and be gay,
> Rage, rage against the dying of the light.
>
> And you, my father, there on the sad height,
> Curse, bless, me now with your fierce tears, I pray.
> Do not go gentle into that good night.
> Rage, rage against the dying of the light.
> (p. 159)

The poem is in form a villanelle. But instead of looking up what that means, get your answer by working out for yourself the exact form of this particular example, its pattern of rhymes and refrains. The villanelle is a fixed form, of French origin, originally reserved for pastoral themes (*villa* = farm or country house). It has often been used for light verse. Thomas may have been attracted to the form's potential in the work of two contemporaries, W. H. Auden and William Empson.

DISCUSSION

Did you work out the pattern? Five three-lined verses are concluded in a quatrain. The first and last lines of the opening verse are repeated alternately as the final line of each of the other three-lined verses, and then brought together to form the concluding couplet of the quatrain. And the whole functions throughout on only two rhymes!

Another point: what happens to the *meaning* of the two repeated lines in the four middle verses, as opposed to their status in the first and last verse? What effect is achieved? Gramatically, it is a simple matter. In the first and last verses, the lines are in the imperative mood ('Do not go gentle . . .'; 'Rage, rage . . .'). In the four middle verses they are in the indicative mood, the mood of simple statement ('Wild men . . . Do not go gentle into that good night' etc.) Such a variation of meaning is obviously one of the attractions of the villanelle form. But what is its particular effect here? I would describe it as follows. The poem is obviously, in terms of its situation, highly personal: a son–father relationship. Two possible dangers suggest themselves. Either an over-personal sentiment if the rhetorical imperative mood were sustained throughout, or a curiously irrelevant argumentativeness if Thomas were simply to insist upon other men's resolution at the approach of death. You may say, that is exactly what the poem does do in its four middle verses. But this is my point. Those four middle verses do take the focus off the father himself – yet not completely, because, though substantially they describe those other men, each of the two refrain lines still seems stubbornly to retain its imperative as well as its indicative mood. So neither the personal nor the argumentative tone becomes absolutely total – giving a logical, and yet a fresh force to the final quatrain, where Thomas most obviously charges his emotional plea. Thomas, like Hopkins, always urged that poems should be read out aloud; and what I've described above is perhaps best tested by just such a reading.

The insistent rhetoric of the poem, however, also owes something to an outside poetic source. Words like 'rage', 'blaze' and 'gay' are insistently Yeatsian ones. 'Gaiety transfiguring all that dread' was how Yeats described the conquering of remorse by heroic defiance in his poem 'Lapis Lazuli'.[5] And Yeats's 'Nineteen Hundred and Nineteen' lists the 'great', the 'wise', and the 'good' who did not see how these qualities, when not strengthened by a more selfish resolve, succumb to contrary historical forces as well as to literal death. ('Come let us mock at the good / That fancied goodness might be gay'.)[6] That particular Yeats poem probably influenced the patterned references of Thomas's four middle verses. Thomas did not need to disguise these verbal and structural parallels because the borrowed rhetoric further disinfects or impersonalizes the poem. The poem is private in a very public way. Even the most personal line – 'And you, my father, there on the sad height' – evokes Shakespeare's Lear and Gloucester. For these reasons, your study of this poem should include comparison with the more completely private 'Elegy' on his father printed at the end of the *Collected Poems* (p. 169).

I also find the poem very rich in oblique meanings. Generally, the later poems do not make such an insistent use of puns and double-meanings as the early ones – which perhaps give them a stronger power when they do occur. Were you aware of any in your first readings of this villanelle? Go over the poem briefly again to see if any strike you. I feel sure a phrase like '*Grave* men, near *death*' made you pause even the first time round (as also in 'A Refusal to Mourn': 'a grave truth').

In fact, that play on the word 'grave' is one I personally wish Thomas had avoided. It's a little too easy (Shakespeare's Mercutio says before he dies, 'Ask for me tomorrow, and you shall find me a grave man').[7] Other oblique meanings seem to me a real enrichment compared to this. Take, in its imperative mood, the line

Do not go gentle into that good night.

'Do not go gentl(y)', certainly. But perhaps also 'Do not go, gentle [ie. gentle one], into that good night': gentle now, in your illness. And look at that 'good night'. A good night, yes, but also a valedictory 'Good Night!' Memories of serious illnesses also remind us of what it is to have 'a good night'. I think these are wonderfully tactful possibilities. And so is this:

Good men, the last wave by, crying how bright . . .

The 'green bay' which follows makes the 'wave' mainly maritime. But something else might flash across our minds – a 'last wave' of the hand. I'll leave you to decide whether these are true to your own reading. One thing is certain. A strict verse-form such as this (one could hardly imagine a stricter) is suited to expressing richnesses in short spaces, richnesses which in turn enliven the essential repetitiveness of the form. We've already seen elsewhere that Thomas is the sort of poet who welcomes technical strictness. (You'll recall, for example, the strict count of syllables in the early poems.) Here,

I think the villanelle form has chastened what must have been in
actuality painful. What strict form does to painful content is
something always worth exploring. John Donne knew it:

> Grief brought to numbers cannot be so fierce,
> For, he tames it, that fetters it in verse.[8]

You might like finally, without too much comment here, to return
to one of the two poems with which you started at the very
beginning – 'The Hunchback in the Park' (p. 104). I don't know what
you thought of it, but I'd like now to suggest that, just as 'After the
funeral', as well as being an elegy for Ann Jones, also involved
Thomas's role as a poet, so 'The Hunchback in the Park' is both about
its ostensible subject and about Thomas's understanding of the poet's
position. In other words, isn't it possible to argue that Thomas
identifies with the hunchback as a type or equivalent of the artist:
isolated, misunderstood, creating something ('a woman figure
without fault') as an opposite to the inadequacies of his own life,
something which survives him? I have an unfair advantage over you
in making this suggestion, which arises from an early manuscript
version where the identification is actually stated ('It is a poem and
it is a woman figure').[9] Perhaps on reflection the poem had already
struck you as something more than a simple piece of reportage. Either
way, re-read it now with this added perspective in mind. Think of
it: Thomas is all at once the poet who writes the poem, one of the
'wild boys innocent as strawberries', and the hunchback himself. And
as preparation for the verbal alertness that the poem might demand,
consider how the phrase 'wild boys innocent as strawberries' was
probably arrived at: through a reversal of the normal idea of innocent
boys and wild strawberries. (Compare 'the man in the wind and the
west moon' in 'And death shall have no dominion'. Or think again
of the phrase 'that night of time' from the first 'Altarwise' sonnet.
It is a 'night of time' because *in* time and because momentous. But
the phrase was produced by reversing a cliché: 'that time of night'.)
A return to 'The Hunchback in the Park' now – as to any of our
poems – should presumably be like Thomas's own return in memory
to that park, a return alert to things not looked for the first time
round.

6. 'Fern Hill' and Later Poems

A chance now to return also to that other poem from the beginning of our study (and itself a poem of beginnings), 'Fern Hill' (1945). We shall here consider it in further detail as an independent major achievement, but also as the poem that stands on the threshold of the last phase (1945–1953) of Thomas's career. As you will have discovered in your first reading, 'Fern Hill' engages a familiar theme, a nostalgic view of innocent childhood. This immediately raises the problem of merely sentimental statement. We clearly would not be much drawn by a poem which merely asserted, notionally, that the child was happy. We would expect such a poem to convince us on the point. So in re-reading 'Fern Hill' now (p. 150) ask yourself how vividly *re-enacted*, and by what means, is the child's experience? Where would you say the adult's different perspective comes most clearly into play? How does the formal structure of the poem work to convey its theme?

DISCUSSION

There is an immediate impression of detailed, but 'easy', excitement, I think you'll agree. It seems relevant that the poem's first word is 'Now', even though it is separated by only two words from 'was'. Indeed, the feeling of pastness tends to fade amidst so much energetically immediate language. A child's psychology seems re-enacted in the poem's very style. Much more insistent than 'was', for example, is a word which is syntactically its main threat – 'And' – a

Dylan Thomas, c.1946
Acknowledgement: The BBC Hulton Picture Library.

word that essentially connects and prolongs, rather than divides and ends. The poem is riddled with 'ands', suggesting a child's accumulative gusto in telling you what matters most. I don't simply mean 'and' as a natural connective *within* a sentence, but as a means of almost making all sentences instantaneously one, and avoiding the force of a full-stop. After all, three fresh verses actually *start* with 'And'. I get an impression of the apparent simultaneity of a child's sensations. Or think of the nice touch in verses 3 and 4 – when the boy goes to sleep the farm isn't merely benighted; it actually goes away. Nothing is truer of a child's way of thinking: things exist *for him*; when he's unconscious they don't exist at all! (You will find the same thing in 'The Hunchback in the Park'. The empty park at night is described as being 'unmade'.) Or look at the word 'lovely', used twice in verse 3: a child's word that Thomas obviously didn't *want* to avoid. Or the nature of the imagination implied in metaphors like 'the tunes from the chimneys' (verse 3, smoke wafting on the air?) and the personified farm with 'the cock on his shoulder' (verse 4). More broadly, one might suggest the affinity the poem has with the cultivated 'naivety' of vision of a painter such as Chagal, whose objects float in a spatial relationship essentially lyrical rather than realistic. The details of 'Fern Hill' can all be realistically explained, but they are caused initially to suggest a floating, merging, and mixing world. For example, it is because the boy is on the hay-waggon in verse 1 that he is able to make 'the trees and leaves / Trail with daisies and barley'; but we experience him doing it *before* we understand how. Again, the 'house high hay' of verse 5: we don't immediately deduce a realistic explanation. The whole scene is not only 'lilting' (verse 1) but tilting, too, in a boy's excited vision. Of course we know that it is a poem of memory, but its real achievement is a re-creative inwardness with what is remembered.

I suppose the first place where we feel a more external comment on the experience is in verse 4, where Thomas says 'So it must have been' – so it must have been in Eden, at the beginning of the world. But Thomas delays any fuller expression of this more external adult perspective until the last verse and a half. I refer not only to the clearer awareness of death and transience there, but to an occasionally more abstract language, as in 'I ran my *heedless* ways' (contrast 'it was running, it was lovely') or the repeated 'Nothing I cared . . .' Incidentally, Thomas remained unhappy about the phrase 'heedless ways', which reminds us that the sometimes necessary abstraction came less easily to him than more concrete imaginings.

Yet perhaps the poem's deepest power comes from the ironic presence of the adult's knowledge even *in* those phrases which made us think mainly, at the time, of the child's innocent sense of boundlessness. I would like you to find your own examples, following from one or two I shall give here from the first verse. That verse is characteristic of the rest in allowing much of the language to come close to the familiarity of cliché ('young and easy', for example, is at only one remove from 'free and easy'). But at times the cliché is already tougher than we think. For instance, the familiarity of *happy as the day is long* lies behind 'happy as the grass was green'. But the Biblical 'As for man, his days are as grass' (*Psalms*, ciii, 15) lies behind both. By changing the cliché, Thomas has made it even less secure. Such an allusion is one we may miss, but having it pointed out suitably alerts us to more than meets the eye. Similarly, in the presence of 'green', the word 'golden' is less a cliché (*golden boy*) than a preview of the autumn which will follow this spring or summer. Or take 'windfall': commonly it connotes unexpected good luck, but the concrete insistence of the verse pushes the cliché back to its original meaning – early-fallen fruit. 'Once below a time', again, may first strike us as mere idle play on the familiar. But the 'below' may not be as innocent as the literal 'under' of 'under the apple boughs' – especially in a verse which has 'night above'. The boy is 'below' (subject to) time – which makes the ideas of climbing, or of being prince and lord, again poignantly insecure. You might now look through verses 2–4 for other such subtly-reverberating phrases.

'Fern Hill' also alerts us to one of the main features of the last poems. We noticed it in 'Poem in October', (see p. 52 above), and it was anticipated to some degree in the earlier 'After the funeral'. I refer to the use of landscape; not in the simple sense that the poems delight in describing nature, though Thomas's descriptive facility certainly comes fully into play in the last phase. The opening of 'A Winter's Tale' (p. 111), for example, will remind you of the atmospheric details of the opening of *Under Milk Wood*. But more important is the way in which nature-description becomes a language for feeling, through which the poet also becomes aware of the essential nature of his religious beliefs. To be more explicit, there is a shift from what we might term a 'materialist' view of nature in the earlier poems to a more conceptual view in the later ones. The 'materialist' view was informed by a moving sense of mystery, but was essentially a vision of organic process. The unstated claim of the earlier poetry seems on reflection to have been that there is around us this organic nature, and we share in it directly through our bodies, and there's nothing else. The more conceptual view is one in which human consciousness itself is now more than merely 'natural', having access to religious concepts and modes of feeling which are then applied *to* nature. The streams in 'Fern Hill' could not think of themselves as 'holy', but that is how they are described. In the earlier poetry it seemed as if this split between 'nature' and 'consciousness' was exactly what Thomas refused to concede.

In 'Fern Hill' Thomas understands, not only the boy's happiness, but also something of its religious implications. Words such as 'mercy', 'sabbath', 'holy', 'blessed', 'praise', 'grace' run through the poem. But in your memory of the poem would you say they added up to a specifically Christian emphasis? I don't think so. From lines and images in such poems as 'A Refusal to Mourn', 'After the funeral' or Poem in October' you will know that Thomas's later poems have a natural tendency to sacramentalize their landscapes. Are the images, then, religiously trivial? My own understanding of 'Fern Hill' would make me say no. What Thomas has stressed there is the harmonious *unity* (not just the magic or unsuspectingness) of the child's vision of the world. And the poem's point, as I see it, is not simply to lament its passing, but to understand that, having been, this vision remains a measuring experience of the value of the created world. That is why this poem's deepest play on the different meanings of a single word comes at its climax:

> Oh as I was young and easy in the mercy of his means,
> Time held me green and dying
> Though I sang in my chains like the sea.

Consider the word 'held'. Because of the 'chains' that follow, it means *fettered*. But because of the 'mercy' that precedes it, 'held' also means *cradled* or *supported*. Time the destroyer is also Time the preserver.

Incidentally, you will find it interesting at some stage to compare 'Fern Hill' with a less rhapsodic treatment of the same farm in the first short story of Thomas's *Portrait of the Artist as a Young Dog*, from which we took that description of the unused front room in Chapter 1. In relation to the poem, you should also bear in mind the very different concerns of 'After the funeral' as a memorial to the Ann Jones who made those farm holidays possible.

Other late poems, such as 'Over Sir John's hill' or 'Poem on his birthday', approach their symbolic landscapes completely from within the adult's full awareness of death. The landscape and its creatures provide what one might call allegories of this awareness. I think you will find that the word 'allegorical' suits, for example, the symbolic use made of the various birds in 'Over Sir John's hill' – where Thomas actually describes himself as 'young Aesop'. But at the same time I'm sure you will also feel that these poems are not merely 'literary' accounts of what the poet sees. The atmosphere of the rural, seaside place where they were written (Laugharne) was probably the greatest single influence on the poet's final work. And you should consider how pervasively this sense of an actual place affects the language and atmosphere of these late poems.

Please now read 'Over Sir John's hill' (p. 152). It is worth responding first of all to its meaning at a simple descriptive level. Then, on a re-reading, ask yourself what the poem says about the fact of death in the natural world. Is it a simple lament? The poet perceives a natural hierarchy in the scene before him: what part has this to play? God is mentioned twice: of what significance is this?

DISCUSSION

The opening lines establish the two images from which two sustained series of metaphors develop. The hawk is 'on fire' (reflecting the sun's last rays, with a sense of apocalypse about him too). And he 'hangs', the first word in a series suggesting execution. The hawk is the executioner of the 'small birds of the bay'. But the language complicates the hierarchy, surely. The hawk itself 'hangs still', is 'noosed', and flies in a 'hawk-eyed dusk' (something is watching him, too). The 'hoisted cloud' of the third line also works two ways: not only is it the crowd of small birds drawn to the hawk's murderous claws, it is the literal cloud in which the hawk itself hangs. The conceit of the hill donning the judge's black cap to pass the death-sentence (verse 2) widens the hierarchy suggested by a court of execution (equipped even with a Clerk of the Court in the form of the poet recording the event?)

  The poem is consistently fanciful in this way. And one particular fancy seems to me important. That is, the fact that the heron is said to grieve over the small birds' death. What are we to make of this? Look at the point where it is first stated, at the end of verse 1. If that were the only occasion, it would surely have a very different effect. The hawk descends to the kill: at the same time the heron stabs at some fish in the river. Momentarily, the idea that the heron is 'bowing its tilted headstone' in grieved homage would be allowed to pass as an innocent fancy. But Thomas goes on claiming that the heron is 'the elegiac fisherbird' (verse 2), that it 'grieves' and 'hymns' (verse 3), that it tell-tales the event (verse 4), and so on. Surely, Thomas would feel as much as we do the self-conscious extravagance of all this. He also knew as well as anyone that the heron is itself a predatory bird. It is possible that, by over-doing the fancy, he is in fact claiming the opposite to the notion that anything in nature 'grieves', either its own or anything else's mortality. By associating himself and the heron as mourners, isn't he, paradoxically, emphasizing that in fact only *man* grieves consciously in the face of mortality? The further effect of this, for me, is to draw attention to other strongly-stated words in the poem. The 'guilt' of the slaughtered sparrows, for example, or their 'souls'. In what sense are they 'guilty', or have souls? These are surely *human* considerations, all the more emphasized as such by being so deliberately and precariously foisted on non-human nature. Similarly, reading 'Over Sir John's hill' on its own, one might even deduce a specifically Christian belief on the poet's part. Yet it is possible to feel that the prayer to God in verse 4 is not as emphatically positioned as the simpler and more characteristic resignation with which the poet ends – engraving, 'before the lunge of the night', the 'notes on this time-shaken/Stone' of the poem. As if the Christian consolation had been more entertained than actually believed in, the poet accepts that all he can really do is record and memorialize.

Please read now 'Poem on his birthday' (p. 155). Its packed detail will demand closer attention on later readings, but what you should aim to get clear first of all are the main stages of its development. At this first approach, also remember the last two points raised from 'Over Sir John's hill': the degree to which human consciousness is foisted on the natural world; and the status of the Christian references.

DISCUSSION

In the last line of verse 2 'Herons, steeple stemmed, bless'. But more characteristic of other creatures around them is that they simply 'spire and spear' or can be thought of as walking 'in their shroud'. (The 'shroud' is a shoal of minnows 'wreathing around their *prayer*', but the whole conceit is stressed as something that the poet 'perceives'.) There is a clear sense in other details of rich but unthinking non-human life. 'Cormorants scud' and flounders and gulls are 'doing what they are told', a phrase the very flatness of which suggests its opposite – that is, action dictated by mere instinct. Flinches now simply fly 'in the claw tracks of hawks'; they don't cry 'Come let us die'. Dolphins 'dive' and don't know that the blood that 'slides good in the sleek mouth' is their own. We are in the world of emblems rather than of allegory. In the meantime, and in contrast, the poet 'celebrates and spurns', 'tolls' and 'toils', 'sings towards anguish', 'perceives', and 'knows'. The first four verses have differentiated between man and nature even while focusing on what unites them: the fact of death.

The next three verses in a sense isolate man even further. (As an exercise, test the italicized paraphrase that follows against your own reading of verse 5:) *In an inner silence (like that under the vault of an arching wave – paradoxically a point of stillness amidst activity and noise) he is conscious of a metaphysical dimension. The 'angelus' bell evokes the idea of the Incarnation, in which God partook of mortal life and death. The 'thirty-five bells' of his own age, however, are made to resound only on the wreckage and failures of a life 'steered', not by faith, but superstitiously 'by the falling stars'. For him, 'to-morrow' is an unknown quantity ('a blind cage') that some actual 'terror' (some historic event?) will open before it is finally and more mysteriously opened by the 'hammer flame' of 'love'. It will be at this ultimate 'unbolting' that he will enter the unknown.*

And this is where (in verses 6 and 7) the exact – or rather, inexact – nature of his religious faith is expressed. This ultimate stage will be a world of 'light', that of some concept called 'God'. But this God is both 'unknown' and 'famous', both a created myth ('fabulous') and yet 'dear'. Similarly, this Heaven 'never was', 'nor will be ever', yet is 'always true'. It is both a 'void' and 'brambled'. But along with this obviously riddling quality goes a more subtle counterpointing. Thus he will be both 'lost' and 'lost/In the . . . light' (a different thing). Again, the light, though 'famous', is 'unknown' perhaps because not consciously knowable (a different thing). *That* could be the sense in which this 'Heaven' will be a 'void'. The picture in verse 7 sees man after death as joining, not only the skeletal remains of birds and mammals, but an 'unborn' God. 'Unborn God and His Ghost' suitably suggests Father, Son, and Holy Ghost before the creation or before the incarnation. But 'unborn' may suggest the *undoing* of God's physical birth as Christ, returning the Godhead to a 'Ghost', just as men to 'spirits' or 'whales' to their skeletal 'roots'. Yet God remains pre-eminent in that hierarchy – as a vague principle of life and 'light' – and every 'soul' remains 'His priest' through the simple fact of existence, an existence that will be now finally 'at cloud quaking peace'. 'Gulled' suggests that any belief in a more personal resurrection will prove to have been intellectual deceit.

'Light' is this 'place' towards which all life moves. 'Dark – that is, ordinary life itself – is the 'way'. And it is a 'long' way. The poet 'knows' that ultimately the 'place' will be a cosmic one (notice the 'stars' of verses 7 and 8), brought about by the end of conscious life, as opposed to material existence. The 'rocketing wind' and 'rage shattered waters' of verse 7 again, however, suggest a man-made apocalypse. But in the meantime, 'on the earth of the night', all he can do is to 'pray . . . faithlessly' to the God who 'is the light of old/And air shaped Heaven' (a Heaven that can only be imagined; cf. 'air-drawn dagger' in *Macbeth*.)

But the prayer moves from mourning (verse 9), to the celebration of the final three verses. The word 'faith' (verse 11) is transferred to 'the whole world', giving it its final meaning as simply the very energy of existence itself. The closer he moves to death, the more intense do the splendours of the natural world become – both in his appetite for them and as if they actually celebrate the very naturalness of his mortality. And in the whole process, he himself also grows to a greater love for other mortals: in verse 8, in a paradoxical phrase, he had been 'alone/With all the living', but in the final verse he sees them as 'angels', 'holier', and 'no more alone'.

On the question of actual beliefs, the poem seems more daring than 'Over Sir John's hill', where the element of 'allegory' remained something of a distancing convention. Ideas and attendant emotions seem here more nakedly open to evaluation. Lines like 'Heaven that never was/Nor will be ever is always true' do yield a logical meaning: 'even if Heaven doesn't exist, man needs to invent it'. But such ideas may still remain open to the charge that their verbal elaboration (like the elaboration of so much else in the poem) covers the absence of any really *complex* meaning. Again, the poem's final vision of a new sympathy for other humans might be thought to lack the grounding in concrete event that we saw in 'There was a Saviour' and 'The tombstone told when she died', or the grounding in actual relationship that we found in 'After the funeral'. On the other hand, like 'Over Sir John's hill', the poem might be thought to have already an adequately powerful theme in its evocation of the burden of human consciousness in a world which otherwise accepts mortality unconsciously.

On the whole, a new reader needs less detailed guidance on these poems from the last phase of Thomas's career. So let us stand back a little from the detail and consider some general views of the kind of poems Thomas was writing at this time. But before we do so it would be useful if you were to familiarize yourself with two more of the relevant poems. Please read now 'In country sleep' (p. 165) and 'In the white giant's thigh' (p. 162). The former may present some initial difficulty because of the syntax of its long wheeling sentences and its accumulation of natural and sacramental images. But its basic situation is simple enough. The poet's daughter, about to go to sleep, is told not to fear the fictional characters of traditional nursery-tales that may fill her young imagination at night-time. The only figure with real power to affect her life is 'the Thief as meek as the dew'. This is Thomas's image for the coming of experience, of sexual awareness, and ultimately of death. But it is not a figure to be feared; it is rather a natural part of the inevitable process of life, seen in the final images of the poem as 'designed' and 'ruled'. For 'In the white giant's thigh' all you need to bear in mind is that the poet is walking on a 'high chalk hill' on which the figure of a huge giant is carved (as at Cerne Abbas in Dorset). Such figures were pagan symbols of fertility. The irony of thus walking, quite literally, 'in the white giant's thigh' is that on the same hill in the poem are buried women who had died childless. Thomas describes their sexual vitality in life, and imagines their yearning for child-bearing fruitfulness as something that survives their death, in the landscape that the poet traverses at night. In reading these two poems now, you will see how their celebration of vitality in the face of mortality ties in with 'Over Sir John's hill' and 'Poem on his birthday'. And in standing back from the detail, we should consider what might account for the consistency of such themes, what characterizes the general tenor of the late poems, and how we might view them in relation to the earlier poetry.

In one sense, consciousness of mortality may have had more than purely personal promptings in this last phase of Thomas's career. Two hints in 'Poem on his birthday' (terror raging 'tomorrow's' cage apart and the 'rocketing wind') may remind us that the historic period of the last phase was one dominated by consciousness of the atomic bomb. In a 1950 broadcast Thomas described the putative scheme for a long poem of which 'Over Sir John's hill', 'In country sleep' and 'In the white giant's thigh' would form separate parts. The overarching structure of the work (the unfinished 'In Country Heaven') involved the inhabitants of Heaven hearing that 'The Earth has killed itself: it is black, petrified, wizened, poisoned, burst; insanity has blown it rotten.'[1] This is a useful reminder of the historic context of poems which don't in any obvious way deal with such realities. But you should consider whether indirect connections between period and poems are not still part of the latter's meaning. And perhaps we should take such connections further back than the very last phase of the career. For example, why should Thomas, during the war, have turned so strongly to the subject of his own childhood – not only in poems like 'Poem in October' or 'Fern Hill' but also in broadcast reminiscences? Mere charges of 'escapism' explain nothing. Is it not possible that such themes, in the context of war, were the result of a search for those experiences that had once suggested that optimism, wholeness, consonance, were not myths but realities? It is significant that Thomas urged the last-minute inclusion of 'Fern Hill' at the proof-stage of *Deaths and Entrances*, emphasizing that it was 'an *essential* part of the feeling and meaning of the book as a whole'.[2] In this, he could only have been relating it to the major emphasis of that volume on the events of war. The connection might also explain the degree to which childhood is not just recalled but strenuously re-enacted. That process was later to be the aim, too, of 'In Country Heaven', whose inhabitants were to 'Live [themselves] back into active participation in the remembered scene, adventure, or spiritual condition'[3] of events on Earth before its destruction.

The main theme of Thomas's work from the wartime elegies on his own childhood through to *Under Milk Wood* is the celebration of innocence. In 'In country sleep' it is the literal innocence of his young daughter. And you may remember the associations of childhood being implied in 'Over Sir John's hill' by the phrase 'the shrill child's play/Wars/Of the sparrows'. But we need not think of innocence only in conventional childhood terms. 'In the white giant's thigh' describes the former sexual frolicking of the childless country women now buried on the hill –

Who once, green countries since, were a hedgerow of joys

– in terms of a natural adult energy that has its own purity. Delighting as it does in such materials, 'In the white giant's thigh' will probably have struck you as more deeply and extensively 'Hardy-like' than 'The tombstone told when she died'. And this is the strain that leads into *Under Milk Wood*, the original idea for which involved the town volunteering to be cut off from the outside world because the 'sanity' that accused Llareggub of being mad was a sanity that accepted infinitely worse evils than the town itself was capable of.[4] We should consider whether the pastoral world created by the later work, soon to appear curiously old-fashioned to the new generation of poets who came into prominence in the 1950s, reflected nevertheless a serious reaction to post-war realities, however indirectly implied. If so, the process may have a parallel in the earlier poetry. The latter's concentration on inner rather than on public certainties may have been partly a reaction to the overbepoliticked 1930s. After all, poems, as well as being texts, have contexts. And in Thomas's case, the periods in which he wrote should not be divorced, either, from the *places* out of which he wrote. Suburban Swansea and, later, even more obscure villages in West Wales bring to mind an essentially *regional* context.

We shall return to suburban Swansea in the next chapter. But we should not too suddenly leave the rural context of the last poems. And the point about using the word 'regional' as well as the word 'rural' is that it evokes a relationship-to-the-centre that is not just a matter of rural-versus-urban. John Wain sees the status of regionalism in Thomas's time as one of the sources of the 'unbearable sadness' of the late poems:

> He grew up in a bad literary period; in some respects, even worse than the one we are in today. For today, at least, there is a general acceptance that Britain is a multi-racial community and there is no pressure on poets to be anything but what they are. In those days there was an untroubled assumption, in metropolitan England, that 'the regions' were dead and had no right to be anything else but dead . . . A less helpful atmosphere for a Welsh poet with a world reputation can hardly be imagined. It constituted a positive guarantee that the world reputation would pull one way, and the Welshness another. So the man, caught between these irreconcilable forces, blesses and mourns.[5]

In the same essay (p. 17), John Wain stresses that 'Thomas's personal symbol for happiness and completeness' is a small rural community, the kind of place described in stories like 'The Peaches' and 'A Visit to Grandpa's' (in the *Portrait*) and in *Under Milk Wood*. The late poems, however, celebrate landscape and geography more than they do community and people. And in saying that, we should realize that relationship and community don't have to be overt themes to be part of the wider meaning of a poem. In making Welshness a landscape, Thomas seems in a broad descent from a particular tendency in Romantic poetry. One thinks of the end of Coleridge's 'Frost at Midnight', of Wordsworth's 'Resolution and Independence', of Keats's 'Ode to Autumn'. Undeniably major poems, they could be said, however, on one view to translate into landscape fears and concerns that as a result remain only vestigially human. In Thomas's own period, Eliot's *Four Quartets* might, in this connection, also come to mind. Comparison of poems which, although different, have potential points of contact, widens our approach to individual texts. For all its stylistic dissimilarity, Thomas's 'In country sleep' relates to Coleridge's 'Frost at midnight', which is also a poet's poem to his sleeping child. Comparing, in turn, both poems with Yeats's 'A Prayer for my Daughter', will also help you judge for yourself the specific issue raised here. We might resist the social and political point of view of Yeats's poem, but the way in which it interrelates nature and society at a particular historic moment offers a useful wider comparison within which to view Thomas's poem.

But this question of community and relationship can also draw its norm from possibilities within Thomas's own achievement. Thus it is possible to feel that 'After the funeral' in 1938 had begun to explore, via Ann Jones, the poet's relationship to a particular culture. And, in a different mood, *Portrait of the Artist as a Young Dog* had celebrated his suburban and rural origins with a strong grasp of roots in a real society. To some degree, these materials had been interrupted by the advent of war, and the poet's return to London. Yet those works are bound to exert some pressure, not only on the late poems, but also on what we take to be the strengths and weaknesses of *Under Milk Wood*, the only late work in which Thomas returned to the theme of community. In its sheer virtuosity, that 'play for voices' may be considered a greater *individual* achievement. But it affords also another example of how the extra-literary 'regional' context is part of the wider unwritten significance of a work. That play seems shaped, not only by the professional demands of radio as a medium, but by the appetite of an 'English' audience for what is essentially a caricature of the Welsh community it evokes. New York's particular appetite for it was London's appetite, writ large at even greater distance from any reality the play could represent. Of course, much in the play's comedy was consonant also with what was most serious in Thomas's attitude – the celebration of colour and vitality. Nor should we forget that these qualities are traditionally most visible in eccentricity; caricature is in any case a mainstream literary method. But this does not close down the question as to what culture or community Thomas could have felt he belonged to at the end, and on which he could draw to secure at least the diversity of any future work. There is a sense of isolation in the late poems, even while they celebrate a rootedness in landscape. You should consider how convincing and meaningful you find the note of celebration bred out of this stance of isolation in 'Author's Prologue' (p. ix), the last completed poem that Thomas wrote. No doubt, ultimately you will want to measure this melancholy isolation against the different, absorbed 'privacy' of the early poems.

At the root of all phases of Thomas's poetry, however, lies his essentially organicist view of life. From the very beginning you have seen him drawn to themes and attitudes that are essentially extra-social. As William Empson put it, 'the point of vision was set too high for him to let the current politics into the structure of metaphors'.[6] We might even be tempted to say 'set too low'. For what might seem to keep ideology, morality, or even ordinary human compassion in any obvious sense out of the poems is Thomas's concern, instead, with organic natural process. In the last poems Thomas clearly relished the scenic materials presented by final settlement in Laugharne. But it should not be ignored how naturally they would have dovetailed into this essentially organicist view of the world, for which, in a sense, the geography at Laugharne simply provided new emblems that happened now to have a local habitation and a name. This was as much a part of the logic of the career as the fact that the early celebration of pre-natal life could take, from 1939 onwards, the birth of his own children as subjects. The late poems seem to take, if anything, even more specifically Christian sources for their imagery. But that the whole enterprise was not in fact orthodoxly Christian was confirmed finally by Thomas's 'Author's Note' at the beginning of the *Collected Poems* where he says that 'These poems, with all their crudities, doubts, and confusions, are written for the love of Man and in praise of God' – but added 'and I'd be a damn' fool if they weren't'. That addition clearly changes the claim. And the defensive ambiguity of the 'Author's Note' was in any case more straightforwardly expressed in conversation with John Malcolm Brinnin, when Thomas said that these were 'poems in praise of God's world by a man who doesn't believe in God'.[7]

But the difficulty of appropriating Thomas for Christianity does not rule out the possibility that his view of life celebrates more than simple animal or organic contingency; that it evinces human values that may have honourable relevance to *any* serious (even 'religious') interpretations of the world. Your own assessment of the poems is bound at some stage to tie in with your valuation of what, in this organicist way, they actually affirm. You'll remember that in connection with 'Light breaks where no sun shines' (above, p. 33) we postponed any actual *evaluation*; it was at the time more important to ask *What*? than *So what*? You'll also remember that what I momentarily queried then was what human consolation it could possibly be to feel that, at death, we rejoin the organic life of the universe as a whole. The late 'Poem on his birthday' begs that question as clearly as the earliest poems. The question itself reminds us that Thomas's relation-to-the-centre was a matter of ideas as well as of geographic or cultural location. The few comments that follow may prompt you to clarify your own view.

We might ask first of all whether the notion of human life surviving death only in some unconscious organic way led the work into expressing cynical or only primitive views of the value of life itself. Speaking of the man he knew, as well as of the work, William Empson spoke up for Thomas's 'keen though not at all poisoned recognition that the world contains horror as well as delight; his chief power as a stylist is to convey a sickened loathing which somehow at once (within the phrase) enforces a welcome for the eternal necessities of the world'.[8] On the other hand, speaking of the work, David Holbrook has argued that it reflects a man arrested psychologically at some disturbed childlike stage that led to regressive attitudes and to an artificially willed poetry.[9] For either view, the evidence of the texture of individual images should presumably be related to the overall tone and development of a poem as a whole. And it is because the organic cycle of process is the nearest thing in Thomas to an overall 'philosophy' that I think we have in some way to measure that as well, and not too easily settle for its being (if it is) simply a convenient affirmative flourish.

It seems to me first of all that it does not in fact cut out from Thomas's view of the world quite ordinary moral responses to tragedy. The emphasis on organic process may have been what kept the wartime elegies from taking, through more direct protest or satire, the kind of collective moral stance we associate with poetry of the urbane centre. But a sense of moral outrage is still powerfully there. Consider the following image from the opening verse of 'Ceremony After a Fire Raid' (p. 121):

> Among the street burned to tireless death
> A child of a few hours
> With its kneading mouth
> Charred on the black breast of the grave
> The mother dug, and its arms full of fires.

It is a real moral emphasis that has brought the baby's 'kneading mouth' (with a suggestion of 'needing mouth') up against the horror of that word 'charred'. The obscenity of unnatural death is highlighted also by the pun on 'dug'. Notice that there is no comma after 'grave' – the punctuation that would have made 'dug' only a noun in apposition to 'breast'. Behind the lines, therefore, lies the norm of *natural* death – the 'grave the mother dug' simply by giving the child life. In the same way, think back to these lines from 'A Refusal to Mourn':

> I shall not murder
> The mankind of her going with a grave truth . . .

The 'mankind' of her going evokes the organic inevitability of any natural death. As Chaucer put it, 'no man may undo the law of kind' – that is, the law of nature. Thomas probably wouldn't have known the Chaucer reference. But a Shakespearean reference is a different matter. In Shakespearean usage 'mankind', when applied to a female, denoted unnatural cruelty.[10] Thomas's usage is slightly different, but it may still draw on Shakespeare. It counterpoints the male atrocity with the femaleness of the victim ('the *man*kind of *her* going'), and in a poem of essentially female kindness ('London's daughter', 'the dark veins of her mother'). The point about not offering a 'grave truth' or 'any further/Elegy of innocence and youth' is that they seem an utterly inadequate response to such an atrocity.

But Thomas's organicist vision may have an even finer claim on our respect. It can be pointed up from even the earliest poem celebrating the organic cycle, 'And death shall have no dominion' (1933, p. 62):

> And death shall have no dominion.
> No more may gulls cry at their ears
> Or waves break loud on the seashores;
> Where blew a flower may a flower no more
> Lift its head to the blows of the rain;
> Though they be mad and dead as nails,
> Heads of the characters hammer through daisies;
> Break in the sun till the sun breaks down,
> And death shall have no dominion.

After we've noted the reworked cliché 'pushing up daisies' in the seventh line here, and after we've noticed that 'hammer' in that line has been suggested by 'blows' and 'nails' in the two previous lines, have we discharged our response and responsibility to what the stanza, and the whole poem, actually implies? Are such clevernesses the *only* thing the poem has to offer? What if we hesitate before dismissing such a theme as mere rhetoric? Obviously, the natural life that continues after the individual's death will not be experienced *by* that individual. And Thomas is careful to say as much (look at lines 2–5). We wonder therefore what consolation it is to say that life goes on. But does the world's delight have meaning only via *personal* needs? Are the wonders of loud seashores diminished because *you* no longer see them? Consider for a moment George Eliot in one of her letters:

> I try to delight in the sunshine that will be when I shall never see it any more. And I think it is possible for this sort of impersonal life to attain great intensity – possible for us to gain much more independence, than is usually believed, of the small bundle of facts that make our own personality.[11]

One unfortunate spin-off from Thomas's stylistic obscurity may
be that when he is *not* obscure he is assumed to be, not just
simple, but simple-minded. I personally don't think that literature
is in any case a vehicle for difficult ideas, as such, certainly not in
the sense of proving or exhausting them. And Thomas is most
certainly not a didactic poet. The full moral complexity of a theme
comes from the reader thinking out the implications of what a
poem has precipitated. You should consider therefore whether
the sheer consistency of this theme in Thomas argues the seriousness,
for him, of just such a view of the 'impersonal' value of the world
that George Eliot puts so memorably. At its very lowest you would
have to concede that it is not nothing; at its highest valuation
it might strike you as a very fine response indeed. Its counterpointing by what is, in Thomas's late poems, also an intensely
personal sadness in the face of death – as in 'Poem on his birthday'.

> Oh, let me midlife mourn . . .
> The voyage to ruin I must run,
> Dawn ships clouted aground—

would surely enrich, rather than diminish, such a theme. As another
poet put it, you have to 'Try and grow used to the place of
every star / And forget your own dark house'.[12] I emphasize the
point about the sheer consistency of the theme in Thomas because
that is what prompts a decision at some stage as to whether it
simply fills a vacuum caused by the absence of other kinds of
moral ideas or is in itself a serious view of life that will not let
him go.

7. Contexts and Conclusions

'I never thought that localities meant so much, nor the genius of places, nor anything like that.' In the biographical outline at the beginning of this *Guide*, we allowed that comment by Thomas to direct us quite simply to events and places. In the meantime, we have encountered strong and often strange poems. We are now in a position to consider the more general contexts contributing to the nature and meanings of those poems. Part of what we mean by 'context' has to do with Thomas's emergence as a poet in what was essentially a Modernist period. And that in turn determines the 'critical' context in which, over the last thirty years, his achievement has been evaluated. But we should not too quickly substitute this sense of time and period for a sense of place and origins. Indeed, we need to keep both kinds of context in play. It will at least have been clear already that in the last phase Thomas was very much a poet of place in literally *scenic* ways. But what about that more complex 'context' – his Welshness? Might it not have been influential earlier in deeper, more hidden ways?

In going back to origins, we can summon up first of all what is still essentially a sense of place. The sentence above about 'localities' came in a letter of 1935 to the closest of his early Swansea friends, the composer Daniel Jones.[1] This letter elegized the fantasticating games, mainly with words, that the two had played on regular evenings in his friend's home, 'Warmley'. Attaching conveniently to that name were also comfortable thoughts about so much of this early world. The first place-within-a-place that any fuller account of Thomas's life would discover is suburbia. The poet's home for the first twenty years of his life was a semi-detached provincial villa, 5 Cwmdonkin Drive, in Swansea. Its modesty did not inhibit a sense of cosiness. But it was a cosiness that, at the time, Thomas was capable of dramatizing in letters as a smugness characteristic of the immediate society that formed his context. This wasn't a smugness seen in relation to Swansea's poorer industrial districts or its 10,000 registered unemployed and 2000 families subjected to the 'Means Test'. It reflected, rather, the imaginative frustrations of being, as he put it, 'at home with the *bourgeoisie*'.[2] Later he could see that the shaping influence of such a milieu was permanent: from the scenic outdoors of Cornwall in 1936 he wrote that 'I stand for, if anything, the aspidistra, the provincial drive, the morning café, the evening pub'.[3] And even then, an early poem such as 'I have longed to move away' (1933; p. 58) already showed that he was half in love with the easeful death represented by suburbia. But at the time it must also have helped to drive him to search for other certainties. He did long to move away.

And before literal escape proved possible, imaginative escape into the privacies of his Notebook poems presented itself. Such a connection (by reaction) between inner and outer worlds might not be brought to mind by the early work of a different kind of poet. But the curious intensities of Thomas's early poems suggest almost an urge to decreate the social world that lay most immediately around him. The earliest Notebook poems (if we ignore what was always an unorthodox way with language) are often *thematically* conventional. But the Notebooks gradually work through such themes as relate (often satirically and bitterly) to an outer world, until they start exploring the strangely unpeopled world of the organic, 'process' poems that we discussed in Chapter 3. Obviously, flight from provincial suburbia won't explain, certainly not on its own, the material strangeness of the poems with which Thomas first made his name. But reference to that context is more fruitful than merely psycho-analytical explanations built on the assumption that Thomas was from the outset a psychologically damaged human being. At least it does not hopelessly confuse man and poems to claim that the latter, in their search for elemental themes and especially in the quality of sexual assertiveness that they show, may have been shaped partly in reaction to the tidy puritanical world around him. It also keeps alive and relevant that part of his 'psychology' that we *are* qualified to identify – his independent, irreverent, 'young dog' personality, so evident in his autobiographical short stories. This factor does not diminish the seriousness of the early poems. But it usefully reminds us that in the kind of provincial obscurity in which he wrote or drafted or initiated, before the age of twenty, nearly a half of the poems that now comprise his final *Collected Poems*, the physical intensity of his themes must have been exactly what enabled him to imagine ultimate recognition and escape.

What I have baldly referred to as his 'unorthodox way with language' may also evoke the Welsh context in a more specific linguistic sense. Thomas's father relayed strong influences into the poet's life. But it is also worth noting something that he did not pass on. That was the Welsh language itself. The father's Welsh was equal to his perfect English, which means that it was in effect his first language. He even taught Welsh in evening classes, and tended to criticize his wife's 'Swansea Welsh'. So both parents were Welsh-speaking. But D. J. Thomas's concern for 'getting on' through education – in which process, in the early decades of this century, the first abandoned ballast tended to be the Welsh language – led him to decide consciously not to raise his son as a Welsh-speaker. The name Dylan, lifted from the Welsh mediaeval classic the *Mabinogi*, would have to suffice. Thus Thomas's only language was English, beautifully enunciated in what he later called his 'cut-glass accent', the result of elocution lessons paid for by his father. But the rural, Welsh-speaking origins from which both parents came (in the old county of Carmarthenshire) could not be completely sealed off. Thomas's regular schoolboy holidays from his earliest years at his maternal aunt's farm, Fernhill, were amongst people whose own daily language was Welsh. Later, Thomas's wife was to say that he had 'the groove of direct hereditary descent in the land of his birth'.[4] She also tended to speak of his 'vegetable background'.[5] More important, along with such roots there went, in both Swansea and Carmarthenshire, a direct living awareness of another language left behind.

The significance of this, though difficult to prove or gauge, is at least likely to be more real than the view of him when being introduced at his first public reading in America – as having come 'out of the druidical mists of Wales'.[6] Yet it isn't a simple case, as is sometimes assumed, of a Welsh-speaker involuntarily reflecting in his English linguistic patterns determined by the Welsh language. By the same token, direct knowledge of the intricate rules of the prosody and internal rhyming patterns of the Welsh poetic tradition is also something that cannot in this case be claimed. Of course, influence from that latter source would not have to involve the kind of detailed knowledge that, say, Gerard Manley Hopkins (who learned Welsh and studied the classic metres) secured. Indeed, Hopkins's own poetry could itself have mediated the influence. Many poets imitated Hopkins in the 1930s, yet they did so in obvious ways that the young Dylan Thomas did *not* follow. (It is Thomas's late poetry that most obviously shows signs of Hopkins.) In the meantime, however, as early as 1934, Thomas was at least capable of claiming that 'I dreamed my genesis' was 'more or less based on Welsh rhythms'.[7] As it happens, the rhythmic oddness of that poem is the result of its regular count of the number of syllables per line. Though this *is* a factor in classic Welsh metres, it does not produce, in any of the many poems that Thomas structures syllabically, any specifically 'Welsh' rhythms. In any case, 'rhythms' are determined more by the internal rules of the actual language used (its syntax, for example) than by externally imposed structures of form. A similar caveat applies to structures other than syllabic ones. Thomas rhymed 'Before I knocked' on 23 words ending in *er* (p. 6); he patterned 'I, in my intricate image' on 72 words ending in *l* sounds (p. 30); and the 102 lines of 'Author's Prologue' rhyme the first with the last line, the second with the 101st line, and so on inwards until the exact centre of the poem is a rhyming couplet (p. ix). Thomas claimed that techniques of this kind 'may be a waste of time for the reader, but not for the poet'.[8] They are obviously very external techniques. At most, such heavy industry provides only an analogy for the meticulous craftsmanship associated with the Welsh poetic tradition, however much it may suggest a particular *kind* of respect for the craft of verse. Thomas certainly had friends who could (and did) tell him as much about the Welsh tradition as he wanted to know.[9] A blurred awareness of alternative models is not in doubt. But to link 'alternative' possibilities to any *detailed* model provided by Welsh literature is not only inaccurate: it obscures possibly deeper aspects of the 'Welshness' of his position and linguistic methods.

Thomas's poems do not have individual Anglo-Welsh linguistic counterparts for, say, the preponderence of present participles that make T. S. Eliot in 'Ash-Wednesday' appear unmistakably an Anglo-American poet. Even language textures stemming from accent or reflecting geography in other ways (such as identify the regional roots of a Wordsworth or a Seamus Heaney) do not have Anglo-Welsh equivalents in Thomas. And yet he may still have taken (even more than those poets) an outsider's advantage of the English language. We might in any case be looking for the wrong thing in searching for specifically 'Welsh' effects. 'Un-English' effects would be a different matter. If we allow our yardstick to be simply a very generalized norm, it is at least clear that Thomas showed an above-average readiness to subvert it. There are moments when an un-Englishness is reflected by individual words which, from the point of view of strict grammar, are not correctly used. We noted the use of 'stringed' instead of *strung* in 'When once the twilight locked no

longer' (see above, p. 36). We can take first of all two further
examples from poems we have already looked at. In 'How shall my
animal' we saw the image of the poet's mouth as 'The invoked,
shrouding veil at the cap of the face'. The mouth would properly
be *invoking* rather than 'invoked'. Similarly, in 'Should lanterns shine'
the lantern's beam was described as an 'unaccustomed light'.
Presumably it would be the objects in the tomb that would be
'unaccustomed' – unaccustomed *to* the light. In both cases, there is
an element of transference, but certainly not of the obvious kind that
we saw in the transferred adjective of 'the dogs in the *wetnosed* yards'
of *Under Milk Wood*. Take again the line from the fourth of the
'Altarwise' sonnets: 'Love's reflection of the mushroom features'. A
previous version shows that its meaning is 'Love [is] reflection'.[10]
Though the contracted verbal form is not incorrect, its odd tone (and
its potential for confusion with the possessive form 'love's reflection')
show Thomas as a willing partner in the eccentric effect produced.
The same is true of this line in 'Poem on his birthday': 'Gulled and
chanter in young Heaven's fold'. The word 'chanter' means a deceitful
horse-dealer, and draws attention to the meaning of being
deceived in the word 'gulled'. But the oddness comes from placing
a past-participle and a noun together that do not play on the same
word. (Compare its difference from, say, *deceived and deceiver* or
chased and chaser; or, if Thomas had wanted only the meaning of
being deceived, *gulled and chantered*.) Although not thinking of
Thomas, F. W. Bateson once commented on a phenomenon that
would seem relevant to Thomas's case: 'The important difference
between the native English writer and the *métèque* (the writer with
a non-English linguistic, racial or political background) is the latter's
lack of respect for the finer points of English idiom and grammar.
This allows [him] to attempt effects of style, sometimes successfully,
that the English writer would feel to be a perverse defiance of the
genius of the language'.[11]

The fluency and idiomatic confidence of Thomas's letters and
prose works show that eccentric effects in the poetry are not
accidentally faltered into. There is, rather, something in his
disposition towards the language that makes him welcome (or at least
causes him not to resist) the off-centre impression that such effects
create. Evidence of his linguistic opportunism is copiously there,
however, even in the letters. These often reveal the kind of objective,
alert wonder that a friend remembers Thomas showing when he
discovered on a restaurant menu that the word 'live' spelt 'evil'
backwards.[12] The letter quoted at the beginning of this chapter
went on to contrast Swansea with 'London, the Academy, and a

tuppenny, half-highbrow success'. The 'half' from the usual idiom *tuppenny-halfpenny* has been cut off to make a new phrase 'half-highbrow'. Another letter has the phrase 'into the littered, great hut', where 'great' has come to mind through hearing *little* in the word 'littered'.[13] This hypersensitivity to accidental meanings created in the flash-points between words is what produces the punning energy of the poems. And we can reasonably speculate that it arises from what is still a certain sense of externality to the English language, a refusal to leave it alone, to take it for granted. An analogy with James Joyce suggests itself: a strong sense of provincial, cultural, even religious, 'otherness' leads to the writer taking revenge as it were (even for the most mixed of motives) on the imperial, standardizing norms of the English language itself.

But one could imagine a darker interpretation of the phenomenon, one that is at least worth mentioning. It would see Thomas in a much more problematic relationship to the dominant literary tradition in which he wrote. It would see his suppressed Welshness in terms of a cultural–linguistic temperament that had been denied its most natural medium, the Welsh language, and thus found in the English language a medium that had to be forced or willed into effects not instinctively natural to it. One fact at least is clear. A particular cultural temperament, whose natural medium is the language that has shaped and expressed it over the centuries, is not itself suddenly extinguished when that language is lost in the first generation. Also relevant is the fact that what is being speculated upon here is the effect, not on the ordinary day-to-day use of the 'new' language, but on its usage under the pressurized conditions of poetry. Under those conditions (the argument would run) Thomas's poetry represents a kind of no man's land between two languages – one dead, the other powerless to be born. Or at least powerless to be born into any kind of natural ease. This would explain not only why he appears so *radically* different from any other poet of the 1930s, but also why he found poetry more and more difficult to write. (What is the significance, for example, of the fact that 'Poem on his birthday' was partly constructed from word-lists drawn from Roget's *Thesaurus*?)[14] It would also explain why his later career depended more on oral performance of poems already accomplished than on the production of new ones – in readings that some would regard as willed and mechanical, as if the product of some struggle between the Welsh and English ('cut-glass') voices. All this might then be taken to explain the 'regressive' impulse in so much of the poetry, not just towards an idealized childhood (from his late twenties) but towards pre-childhood states at a much earlier age.

A poetry of adulthood (the theory would run) was peculiarly difficult since, culturally, it could not be a Welsh adulthood. Consequently he found less and less to write about that was not connected with the fact that he was not a child and wouldn't live for ever.

Such a view runs at least two risks. First, the danger of sounding plausible on the failures and deficiencies but without (from the same negative base) being able to account for the obvious successes and merits. Secondly, the danger of patronization, of attributing to a theory of linguistic damage effects whose wider context includes also the new adventurousness that accompanied poetic Modernism. This is a context to which we shall return. Its relevance, however, will be to larger aspects of style than just the verbal inventiveness that we've noted so far. In the meantime, the negative view outlined above usefully reminds us how descriptively thin is the standard explanation 'provincial' on which we tend to fall back in labelling writers whose roots lie outside the centre. Real cultural tensions are likely to be there, however difficult they may be to describe, tensions all the more likely to be intensified when an alternative language is also involved. What is also brought home is the way Thomas's poetry has been, and still is, appropriated by more politically powerful cultures, so that only abstract idealizing accounts of it become possible.

Nevertheless, it is in the sharpening of a certain external opportunism that the context of a different culture, centering also on a different language, is most obviously manifest. It is clear that a good deal of Anglo-Welsh literature in the relevant part of this century, even in the form of the novel, and in the hands of Welsh and non-Welsh speakers alike, showed a relish for what is, in terms of linguistic and stylistic effects high-definition performance. The phenomenon has analogies also in the spheres of broadcasting and acting styles in the same period and in the case of personalities from the same kind of background as Thomas. Though it is a spin-off from genuine cultural difference, we don't have to pursue explanations back to deep atavistic roots. What is relevant is the Welshman's impulse to draw on the differences that help him gain visibility and identity in an essentially centralized Britain. To find, in poetry, any linguistic equivalent from within a completely English situation we would have to imagine a period like that of Shakespeare's England when the language was in a state of flux, presenting Shakespeare with the opportunity of stamping his own will upon it. Hopkins, doing similar things with languages, did so at a time when the same sanction of flux did not obtain. Hopkins's sanction came from more external accidents: his own non-publishing obscurity and (interestingly enough) his perception of alternative possibilities in the structure and poetic tradition of the Welsh language. The latter source, as we have stressed, was only a vague prompting for Thomas. But personal obscurity doesn't have to take the form of the literal seclusion of the Jesuit Hopkins or of the reclusive Emily Dickinson to leave a mark. And an added fact is that the ordinary provincial obscurity out of which Thomas first wrote was also in one sense prolonged. His English poetic contemporaries took the usual route through university. To have followed an equivalent route might have influenced the themes as well as what we can call the stylistic accountability of Thomas's early poems. His different situation probably also prolonged the phase in which themes were determined by an essentially adolescent sensibility. The word 'adolescent' need not be any more pejorative than a view of early Auden as exhibiting an essentially 'undergraduate' sensibility. Indeed, it would be an appreciative view of Thomas's early poems that saw them as articulating, at base, what it feels like to be an adolescent; a good deal of his originality comes from that fact. And one can imagine that his situation promoted opportunities for what was stylistically as well as thematically private.

It is important to bring style and theme together. As already noted, the earliest Notebook poems were thematically conventional. They were also stylistically so. And it is important to remember that, at all stages of his career, Thomas could write lucid, direct poems; more than that – lucid, direct and *accomplished* poems:

> Paper and sticks and shovel and match
> Why won't the news of the old world catch
> And the fire in a temper start . . .
>
> Sharp and shrill my silly tongue scratches
> Words on the air as the fire catches
> *You* never did and *he* never did.

'Paper and Sticks', from which those stanzas are taken, was even included in *Deaths and Entrances*. The fact that it was later replaced by 'Do not go gentle' in the *Collected Poems* draws attention to Thomas's own concern for poems that were more individually characteristic. 'Paper and Sticks', like so many poems he left unpublished, or published but left uncollected, seems to use some kind of borrowed voice. Thomas realized early what exactly represented his own voice – when he selected the eighteen poems that he did select for his first volume. The choice at that stage was relatively straightforward: he selected the eighteen from amongst the most recent of his poems. These combined private organic themes with what was then a relatively new textural density. But even less dense earlier poems that went from the Notebooks into the second and third volumes were also obviously chosen because they already showed development towards this characteristic intensity of theme and style. In reality, 'Paper and Sticks' was the only poem ever allowed to break so completely (although only momentarily) the consistency of idiom to which Thomas wanted to give 'collected' permanence. The style of the later poems had to develop out of that of the earlier, as less private subjects demanded attention. Yet we have seen a consistency in the themes that those subjects brought out. And even the ultimate replacement of dense, extended images by verbal and musical accumulation in later poems still showed a concern for the weight and density of the whole. Thomas himself obviously found such development difficult: 'I'm almost afraid of all the once-necessary artifices and obscurities, and can't, for the life or the death of me, get any real liberation, any diffusion or dilution or anything, into the churning bulk of the words.'[15] In returning here to the 'artifices and obscurities' of the early poems, we should consider again their exact nature, why they were difficult to escape from, and why they were considered 'once-necessary'.

We can start with that point we made about some of Thomas's poems using something like a borrowed voice. It seems clear that the direct voice of a poem such as 'Paper and Sticks' (as if in some other poet's style) bears no relation to Thomas's real needs. As it happens, John Bayley has claimed that a certain ventriloquial clarity 'pops out' at us in lines even in some of the dense, most characteristic poems.[16] Bayley's point, however, is not just about clarity. Such a line as 'To surrender now is to pay the expensive ogre twice' (p. 87) has more importantly a kind of uncharacteristic authorial knowingness about it. This contrasts with what Bayley sees as the more genuine identity of the characteristic Thomas style. That identity comes from a language that is more the expression of the poet's almost physical feel of his own selfhood than it is a 'comment on' experience or a 'description of' its ostensible subject. It is as if the poet is most genuinely himself when at a remove from a style that conveys opinions, mediates traditional emotions, or manifests self-possession. This presumably explains why Thomas's early themes are essentially few: his song is in any case ultimately of *himself*. Though in a sense this remained true of the whole career, Bayley finds what he calls the 'trapped effectiveness' of the best early poems more impressive than what he sees as the more open, plangent commentaries of the later ones. The early poetry, then, closes the traditional gap between poet and poem.

It also closes the usual gap between word and thing. Often, the words don't seem referentially to *indicate* things as much as *become* things themselves. To some degree, I feel it is easy to over-emphasize this aspect. A phrase like 'brambles in the wringing brains' (p. 6) certainly makes us feel the sensation *in* the words. But there is much less of this purely mimetic effect in Thomas than in, say, Hopkins. However, another example from Thomas may suggest why we always feel that there is more of it there:

> The bagpipe-breasted ladies in the deadweed
> Blew out the blood gauze through the wound of manwax.
> (p. 67)

Isn't the 'thinginess' of these words the result of our not quite knowing in the first place what the things are that they communicate? Isn't it the strangeness of the referents that gives such apparently autonomous life to the words? It is as if the poet who evacuated his poems of the social world around him, and who seems most characteristic when he reveals his own sensibility rather than when he articulates ideas or opinions, is also attracted by material which, because of its strangeness, makes thing and word appear to become one.

The strangeness of his material also bears on the question of syntax. We have already seen that Thomas's syntax can be difficult. But the critic Donald Davie has gone further, and claimed that what we often get in Thomas is 'pseudo-syntax', 'a play of empty forms'. Davie quotes from the seventh of the 'Altarwise' sonnets (p. 68), as follows:

> Time, milk, and magic, from the world beginning,
> Time is the tune my ladies lend their heartbreak,
> From bald pavilions and the house of bread
> Time tracks the sound of shape on man and cloud,
> On rose and icile the ringing handprint.

Davie comments on that penultimate line: 'The verb "tracks" is completely void of meaning. What appears to be narrative ("Time", the agent, transfers energy through "tracks" to the object "sound") is in fact an endless series of copulas: "Time is tracking which is sound which is shape . . ." and so on.'[17] Alastair Fowler countered: 'One is irritated into replying. "The verb 'tracks' is *not* devoid of meaning: prove that it is".'[18] But Davie's point is at least wider than just our difficulty in working out the syntax. His argument is that Thomas's sentences only appear to drive on through their verbs; that, although 'formally correct, his syntax cannot mime, as it offers to do, a movement of the mind'. Clearly, Thomas's style would not be a good one in which to write the minutes of a committee meeting! But surely the strangeness of a poem's materials or events is bound to have some bearing on the genuine expressiveness or otherwise of its syntactic forms. We could argue that the logic of the events and the logic of grammar are being suspended for something like the same motive.

Let us explore the point further by noting first of all that Davie has wrongly punctuated the first line of his quotation from the 'Altarwise' sonnet above. Davie ends that first line with a comma whereas Thomas in fact ended it with a full-stop. Therefore that line syntactically belongs to what has gone before, not to what Davie quotes here! Yet the interesting thing is that one can see how easy it would be to make that misquotation. That first line does indeed appear to lead fairly happily into what follows. And it does so precisely because of the repetitive, appositional nature of Thomas's syntax. The line already has some kind of ghost-relationship to what follows. Davie himself notes the characteristic stylistic effect of what he calls 'simultaneity and identification', but doesn't like it; it abandons, he says, the 'intelligible structure of the conscious mind'. Yet simultaneity and identification are the *theme* as well as the style of these sonnets (we saw as much when we looked at the first two sonnets in Chapter 4 above). Of course, style in poetry doesn't always have physically to mime meaning. If it did so, it would be too much a case of killing one bird with two stones! But it should at least be noted that in the specific line whose main verb Davie finds 'completely void of meaning',

Time tracks the sound of shape on man and cloud,

what is being mimed is already a strange and difficult abstract idea – that of the simultaneity of time and space. 'Time tracks the sound of shape on man and cloud' is Thomas's way of expressing what Time is: Time is imaginable only in terms of the sound and shape of *things* – things that are not abstract, and that move ('cloud'), fade ('rose'), and melt ('icicle'). Time 'tracks' these things both in the sense of creating the sad music of their mortality (the 'sound' or significance of their shapes) as on a *sound-track*, and also in the sense of *tracking them down*. The reality of abstract Time is simultaneous and identical with the physical things it destroys. Ironically, Davie seems close to the truth even in the dismissive parody he offers: 'Time is tracking which is sound which is shape'. Our concern at present is the nature of the syntax, rather than the ramifications of meaning. But the way in which the two are always interrelated in Thomas is at the heart of our experience of reading his densest poems. Donald Davie would also argue that Thomas's syntax and rhythm do not create enough ventilation around the images to ease the act of reading (as opposed to the act of explicative commentary). And there is a good deal of truth in this. But it is surely not the same thing as saying that 'tracks' is 'completely void of meaning'.

This effect of simultaneity produced by the syntax is widespread. And more interesting, for example, than Thomas's frequent delaying of a main verb or of a verb's object are the ghost-clauses that such delay is allowed to activate. Take the following lines from another poem:

> Hold hard, these ancient minutes in the cuckoo's month,
> Under the lank, fourth folly on Glamorgan's hill,
> As the green blooms ride upward, to the drive of time;
> (p. 44)

In these lines we are bound to hear *Hold hard these ancient minutes* as a main clause, even though the commas show that the real main clause is 'Hold hard . . . to the drive of time'. And before we've grasped as much, we will also have heard (as a complete syntactic unit, despite the comma) *As the green blooms ride upward to the drive of time*. Compare King Lear's lines, 'Behold yon simpering dame,/Whose face between her forks presages snow'. We know that it is the look on the woman's face presaging sexual frigidity ('snow between her forks [legs]') that is the main meaning. But Shakespeare's syntax also makes us see her *face between her forks*. Similar ghost-effects of syntax occur too often in Thomas to be mere accidents. He seems bent on accommodating them. They are a kind of syntactic pun. And this is related to the visual strangeness of his material in the first place. Just as, within that given strangeness, we are not allowed to have any ordinary expectations of what we hope to find – so also are we not allowed to expect a syntax that will take the shortest route, or a route in only one direction. The skeleton of main clauses is there, but heavily encumbered with subsidiary and appositional units. And we can imagine how such a syntax is made necessary also by what we saw Thomas claim to be his method with images: 'A poem by myself *needs* a host of images . . . I make one image, – though "make" is not the word, I let, perhaps, an image be "made" emotionally in me and then apply to it what intellectual and critical forces I possess – let it breed another, let that image contradict the first, make, of the third image bred out of the other two together, a fourth contradictory image, and let them all, within my imposed formal limits, conflict'.[19]

Again, the whole enterprise argues a certain 'external' feel for the opportunities of the language. And this impression remains in the effect of the whole. On the question of syntax, not even a reading-aloud could bridge the syntactic delays and tangential phrases of the densest early poems in a way that would give them idiomatic naturalness. (A good example on which to test the truth of this would be 'I, in my intricate image', p. 30.) In the opening lines of Hardy's 'A Broken Appointment', or even of *Paradise Lost*, the spoken voice can redeem the syntactic delay by emphasizing the main verb when it is reached. In Thomas, this syntactic pointing would have to be done too often, in the midst of other diversions caused by ghost-clauses, and against the background of already obscure material. Though this is not true of all early poems to the same degree, its logic and significance are general. Despite their obvious musicality, the early poems, from the point of view of what sense demands, are designed first of all as if for solid existence on the page. The poems are heavy with trapped possibilities, at one remove from what the spoken voice could release. It may be significant that Thomas's own later readings did not include many of the early poems and, apart from the first 'Altarwise' sonnet, none of the densest ones. What made the later poems more suited to public readings was exactly the degree of 'dilution' he had managed to achieve in them, in syntax as well as image. Yet the logic of the whole career still came from the very poems that needed such dilution. And it is paradoxical that what is most deeply revelatory of the man himself is, in those early poems, inextricably tied in with strange narratives and irreducible images and syntax. This suggests again his situation as one writing from outside the English centre. From the beginning, his eye was on London publication, but in mediating his themes indirectly in this way, Thomas seems to have felt free to bear an actual reading audience only vaguely in mind. It is as if the Welshman was preserving his sense of his own identity as man and poet by subverting the cultural expectations normally associated with the English tradition. His apology might be that

> It is impossible to say just what I mean!
> But as if a magic lantern threw the nerves in patterns on a screen . . .

But evoking T. S. Eliot's 'The Love Song of J. Alfred Prufrock', the first great Modernist poem in English, is also relevant in another way. For what impelled the early Thomas to write as he did is unlikely to have been only his Welsh or 'outsider' relationship to a central English tradition. That is not to say that we should underestimate this 'outsider' situation in the incentive and opportunity it gave him to forge his own idiom. Indeed, in turning now to the wider influence of the Modernist atmosphere in which he first wrote, we should remember that the prime exemplars of poetic Modernism (Pound, Eliot, the later Yeats) were themselves not English. Their freedom to change the nature of poetic expression came from something like the same cultural independence. The major relevance of a figure like Eliot (whom Thomas consistently admired) did not lie in an urge to copy him directly, even though Thomas's early Notebook poems do show Eliotian touches, just as an early schoolboy essay showed a precocious awareness of the poets and the kinds of experimentation that went to the making of 'Modern Poetry'.[20] Thomas would not have been interested in all of the theory or rationalization that went along with poetic Modernism, and the seedy urbanism or allusive metropolitanism we associate with its leading products are at a distinct remove from Thomas's themes of organic process. Indeed, some of the techniques and forms central to the shaping of Modernist poetry (brief Imagist-type lyrics and impressionistic free-verse patterns) were the very things left abandoned in the early Notebooks when Thomas discovered his own characteristic voice. Yet, even having turned to more private themes and to heavily-designed stanzaic forms, he may well have consciously hung on to, and intensified, what any young poet would have perceived as the main object-lesson of Modernism: concreteness of presentation. And in this, influences from an earlier age that were acclimatized *because* of Modernism, even if they were subsidiary or late influences on Modernism itself, would also have been freshly potent. Thus Thomas acknowledged the influence not only of Imagist poets but of Elizabethan and Jacobean dramatists and the Metaphysical Poets, influences that Eliot himself had made freshly current. And even if, looking back later at such influences, Thomas saw 'no Hopkins',[21] that poet must also surely have been part of what was in the air around 1930. Indeed, Hopkins's influence, ranging from pastiche to subtler responses, was heavier on the poets of the thirties than on the first-generation Modernists such as Pound and Eliot, whose styles had been formed before Hopkins's publication in 1918. The young Thomas was fully aware of Hopkins, and it is to his credit that he did not adopt the most obvious Hopkinsian effects as tricks. But a less superficial influence could still have been a more important one, validating a respect, not only for concreteness of image, but for the weight and density of the whole movement of verse. Thomas is Modernist in his acceptance of the final barrier that Modernism itself in this sense had placed against any return to Victorian discursiveness or Georgian descriptiveness. And of course another Modernist trait that he absorbed was the conscious foregrounding of language as language, language itself as theme, within poems.

Yet if we take the two key aspects of Modernist poetry to be Imagism and Symbolism, Thomas's aims were clearly less modest than the former and probably less ambitious than the latter. And in both cases his actual material has a good deal to do with the difference. Ezra Pound defined an 'Image' as 'that which presents an intellectual and emotional complex in an instant of time'.[22] The aim was to give such 'Images' in poetry something approaching the instantaneous completeness of communication we associate with sculpture or painting. The first of three principles of Imagism, formulated in 1912, explained that the 'thing' the image communicated could be either 'subjective' or 'objective'; that is, it need not be a rendering without a point of view.[23] But no attempt to communicate the significance of the experience created must be allowed to take the language far from the rendered image itself. So a typical Imagist poem did little more than present a series of clear pictures. Thomas would clearly not be satisfied with the small compass that such an enterprise allows, and he satirized wickedly the unadventurousness of poems in this tradition.[24] But the taboo on commentary as such is not unrelated to his own methods. The difference is that, in his case, a strong *narrative* emphasis links, and takes us through, the images. His images are also themselves energetic actors, locations or events in that narrative (not simply 'things' mediated or mediated upon) and come from strange landscapes.

When we turn to Symbolism, it is again from the point of view mainly of contrast, though there are some connections which will help us focus further what Thomas does in his own way. For all that Thomas called himself 'the Rimbaud of Cwmdonkin Drive',[25] his knowledge of the *Symboliste* poetry of late nineteenth-century France was at best negligible. His fondness for synaesthesically mixing the senses ('The whispering ears will watch love drummed away') may have come from Rimbaud, via translation, but is in itself no stranger than many other effects in his work. It is in any case the legacy of *Symboliste* method in Yeats or Eliot that probably counted. Two of its main features seem worth evoking.

First, the *musical* implications of the Symbolist ideal of living in a world of words. Paul Valéry had claimed that what the poet did to ordinary language was to 'musicalize' it. This meant not just poetry's usual capitalization on the sounds of words, but a determined attempt thereby to deny that the most important function of language comes from its referential or denotative power. Thus aspiring to the condition of music, Symbolist poetry sought to express states of feeling directly, allowing language to negotiate referentially with the world as little as possible. One can see why this should remind us of Thomas, the poet most often accused of writing musically without sense. And even a friendly critic can see that Thomas promotes, sustains, and elaborates the musical potential of his words. But non-referentially? Surely Thomas's narratives are busily descriptive of *things*, however strange. And a further consideration is the question of the rhythmic impression of the whole. *Symboliste*-influenced poems, like so many by the early Yeats, match their ethereal language with moody, hesitant, hovering rhythms. Yeats himself in this early phase had urged that poets should 'cast out of serious poetry those energetic rhythms, as of a man running, which are the invention of the will with its eyes always on something to be done or undone'.[26] There are indifferent poems in Thomas's juvenilia, even in his early Notebooks, that would seem in accord with this advice. But the only mature poem with anything like a world-weary *Symboliste* music is 'We lying by seasand' (1937, p. 75). Its opening, characteristic of the whole, shows the *Symboliste* trick of promoting an aetherial effect by muting the tangibility of things and rhythms:

> We lying by seasand, watching yellow
> And the grave sea, mock who deride
> Who follow the red rivers, hollow
> Alcove of words out of cicada shade,
> For in this yellow grave of sand and sea
> A calling for colour calls with the wind
> That's grave and gay as grave and sea
> Sleeping on either hand.

This, surely, isn't characteristic Thomas. Indeed, the characteristic Thomas might even deserve Yeats's accusation against 'energetic rhythms' or against 'the will with its eyes always on something to be done or undone'. So far, then, the poet who in one of his own short stories exclaims 'Image, all image'[27] would seem more amenable to Imagist than to Symbolist ideals. But certain other potentials in Symbolist Modernism (there only in miniature in Imagism) might have been influential. Such influence might not be a case of copied models, but an awareness of new kinds of structural freedom. One Symbolist effect, sanctioned preeminently by Eliot's example, was the effect of discontinuity. Since this has often, in Thomas's case, been laid at the door of Surrealism, we should consider that accusation first before returning to the kind of discontinuity that a poet such as Eliot employed.

Obviously, much in early Thomas smacks of Surrealism and there can be no doubt that a certain kind of image took some of its flavour from such writing. But Surrealism proper is not defined by *kinds* of imagery. Its hallucinatory effect comes from the odd *relationship* of images, unselected and irrationally juxtaposed. David Gascoyne, a Surrealist poet and contemporary of Thomas, defined such poetry as 'a perpetual flow of irrational thought in the form of images'.[28] Like the Surrealists, Thomas thought of himself as drawing on subconscious material. But whereas the Surrealists allowed no room for the selection, control, and development of images, Thomas again seems busy with those very activities, and with everything carefully subjected to the aesthetic demands of poetic form. Take the opening verse of 'When, like a running grave' (p. 16):

> When, like a running grave, time tracks you down,
> Your calm and cuddled is a scythe of hairs,
> Love in her gear is slowly through the house,
> Up naked stairs, a turtle in a hearse,
> Hauled to the dome . . .

A 'running grave', a 'scythe of hairs', a 'turtle in a hearse' seem, on their own, suitably Surrealistic. But even in this obscurest of poems we feel that the connections are being made for us, and the images consciously developed. It is a poem argued (or rather a narrative enacted) completely through images, so it is almost impossible to paraphrase, but the images are certainly not left in only a one-off juxtaposition to each other. Thus we later see (via an image of a cinder track) why Thomas wanted to say 'time *tracks* you down'. Again, it is clear later that a 'running' grave was in any case meant (like a running sore) to suggest infection and disease. The 'scythe of hairs', on reflection, is that which scythes hairs. The verb 'is' in the third line is consciously made to have the ghost-effect of a complete positive action ('*is* slowly through the house') before we realize that it is in fact a subsidiary verb in a passive action ('is . . . Hauled'). 'Hearse' makes 'gear' mechanical, but 'tailor' later also makes it an image of clothes (as in *night-gear*); and in the meantime the idea of clothes has made the stairs 'naked'. The wit in describing uncarpeted stairs as 'naked' is also that which puts the slowest animal ('turtle') in the slowest vehicle ('hearse'). One feels that there might be no end to the ingenuity, and all this is certainly no defence of the poem's ultimate obscurity. But not only is Thomas's comment about letting one image 'breed' another, even while allowing them to contradict, a fair description; it describes a method that has by no means surrendered 'intellectual and critical forces' to automatic writing.

It would be difficult to imagine two more dissimilar poets than Eliot and Thomas. Yet the revolution effected by Eliot was for many very different younger poets a point of no return to older ways of writing. It was not a matter of copying him. Thus it is not Eliot's techniques of discontinuity as such that make him more relevant than Surrealism here. It is, rather, the fact that this particular aspect of Symbolist method helped promote a view of poems as autonomous or irreducible semantic worlds. This view in Thomas will bring us back ultimately to what he meant by saying that his early poems were to be read 'literally'. So it is worth instancing first of all what kind of image or symbol, quite apart from what kind of complete poem, could be thought of as being irreducible. Take Yeats's images of the chestnut-tree and the dancer at the end of 'Among School Children', for example. It doesn't seem adequate to call them metaphors. Why? Because there are no separate literal things that momentarily we are invited to see differently by having them called a chestnut-tree or a 'body swayed to music'. In the same way, they are not 'symbols' in the traditional sense in which a symbol permanently 'stands-in' for a thing or a concept, is an ingredient in a complete allegory, or can be unpacked back into what the poet is 'really' writing about. No other things into which the images might be translated are any better, or more real, examples of what is being communicated than the chestnut-tree and dancer already are. They are irredeemably themselves; they are literal. Now, the rest of 'Among School Children' is quite ordinarily descriptive and meditative, and has raised modes of feeling or ways of seeing that provide the logic of those final images. But what if it hadn't? What would it be like, within a poem, to move *only* amongst irreducibly literal images that nevertheless seem to have the kind of air of significance about them that tempts us (unhelpfully) to unpack the poem like a suitcase? Such a poem would surely parallel even more Dylan Thomas's kind of obscurity if it also – like Yeats's 'Byzantium' for example – completely inhabited an already strange landscape.

That possibility of a *complete* poem being irreducible (of being Symbolist rather than symbolical) is something we encounter particularly in Eliot's earlier verse. The world of such a poem need not be a strange one. *The Waste Land* (1922), for example, presents us in the main with recognizable social or geographic scenes. They can involve difficulties presented by smaller-scaled literary and cultural-historical allusions, and can even be disconcertingly interrupted by these. But our main difficulty comes from the apparent *discontinuity* between the main scenes, or between the various sections of the whole poem. Narrative or descriptive continuity has been ignored. *The Waste Land* deserves the description once offered of a Symbolist poem as one in which symbols are ranged around and the 'meaning' flowers from the spaces in between.

Now, *The Waste Land* is uncompromisingly discontinuous at the ordinary level of narrative. Once again (as with 'The Love Song of J. Alfred Prufrock') lines from within the poem perfectly express our experience of reading the poem itself – 'Son of man, you cannot say or guess/For you know only a heap of broken images'. The strong emphasis on at least *narrative* continuity in Thomas sets him at a great remove from such a phenomenon as is represented by *The Waste Land*. But the degree of discontinuity need not be as extreme as that, even in Eliot. Indeed, that degree of discontinuity is made both necessary and effective only by the special needs of writing a *long* poem in the Symbolist mode. Eliot's shorter earlier poems, however, also make surprising leaps or rapid, unexplained transitions that are designed to prevent them from 'adding up' in conveniently tidy ways. Thus the Jamesean social materials of 'Prufrock' tempt us to reduce that poem back into some descriptive narrative of an orthodox realistic kind: as if what Eliot had done was imagine such a narrative, and then write it out more challengingly by omitting the connections, or blurring the realism. But if we do such unpacking, the narrative we are left with (though it *is* partly evoked) cannot account at all for the particular resonance of the poem itself, and would locate the poem more firmly in a merely realistic world than it appears to want. Such difficulties are raised even more strikingly by other Eliot poems such as 'A Cooking Egg' and 'Mr Eliot's Sunday Morning Service'. Donald Davie has persuasively argued that the strange coexistence in those poems, of objects not normally thought of as being associated, can only be understood if we accept that Symbolist poems are not cryptic versions of realistic narratives.[29]

Such writing must have brought about a sea-change in what younger poets perceived as allowable possibilities. Even W. H. Auden (whose poetry is more leisurely and discursive than Thomas's) told Nevill Coghill that the right way to construct a poem was through the organization of logically-discontinuous images à la *The Waste Land*. The technique is visible in a poem such as Auden's 'Now the leaves are falling fast', from a period contemporary with Thomas's *18 Poems*. And the influence on Thomas can be gauged by the delight with which, in an early letter of 1934, he quoted Eliot on the poet's new freedom from constraints of 'meaning' of a traditional kind: 'Some poets, assuming that there are other minds like their own, become impatient of this "meaning" which seems superfluous, and perceive possibilities of intensity through its elimination.'[30]

But Thomas would seem, more than any poet of his generation, to have seized on Modernism's sanctioning, not only of the discontinuity of disparate images, but also of the irreducibility that comes from a relentless concreteness of presentation. And if we now return to what Thomas meant by saying that his poems were to be read 'literally', we can see a wide variety in the implications of that term. Let us first of all consider the irreducible literalness of individual images. It seems clear, doesn't it, that when Thomas says 'The ball I threw while playing in the park/Has not yet reached the ground' we would be foolish to want the park or the permanently suspended ball to 'represent' other things. The unstated logic of the poem allows us to negotiate the symbol (as with Yeats's chestnut-tree and dancer) without unpacking it. We can talk of its meaning certainly, but would be foolish to think that the items in the symbol stand for other things. Even when the items evoke a less familiar landscape, the same air of irreducible literalness applies. So we would also be wrong to hold back literal assent even from such lines as 'Above the waste allotments the dawn halts'. As we have seen in that particular poem, the 'dawn' is already a metaphor of a traditional kind: it is the 'dawn' or 'light' of consciousness; it *does* stand for something else. Here, surely, we get our bearings from recognizing that there is indeed some measure of point-for-point equivalence. And this is fine – as long as we recognize also that the aim of the poem ('Light breaks where no sun shines') is to make us delight in the independent literal life that the metaphor has been allowed to achieve. The point is that we don't feel we *want* to translate the lines back to other referents; we have come to read even recognizable metaphors as if they were *themselves* 'literal'.

Determining the difficulty raised by all this is the degree to which the opening of a poem reveals the ostensible area in which it is working. Despite its strong and original phrasing, the opening

Before I knocked and flesh let enter,
With liquid hands tapped on the womb
(p. 6)

reveals its subject as prenatal life quite directly. The outer circumference of the poem, as it were, is established – and there is a sense in which all the particularizing images that follow are indeed metaphors, and known to be so, because we don't lose sight of that outer circumference. But it is another thing when a poem starts by thus denoting its area of reference but then develops *only within* the independent logic of its original metaphors. Different again is the case of the poem 'The spire cranes' which *starts*, and continues, only with metaphor. The irony is that the majority of Thomas's early poems allow us, in these different ways, to speak, if we must, of ordinary metaphor. It is when such metaphors become the very foreground of the poem, as it were, that the term seems inadequate; or (to change our own metaphor!) when the poem seems to have been turned inside-out; that is to say, when the normally inward secret comparisons that we think of metaphor as being become the main outward life of the poem. In such cases, the 'real' referents in the actual world seem almost like 'other' things to which this 'literal' narrative is compared.

But it is yet another thing when Thomas writes out a narrative that has just never *had* a real-world equivalent that could stand as referent in the first place. That, surely, is what we saw in the 'Altarwise' sonnets. And to that extreme example we can add such poems as 'Where once the waters of your face', 'When, like a running grave', 'I fellowed sleep', and 'I', in my intricate image'. They don't have what we've called an outer circumference or outer reference, like pre-natal life or the process of birth. Yet isn't language without reference, by definition, nonsense? Yes, it is. But we must remember that it is *narrative* without reference that we are talking about. In the last poems mentioned it is the *events* described that have no equivalents in the real world. Yet, it follows that their individual words or images don't need defending against the charge of being non-referential or of being only spuriously literal. The realities they refer to (realities like 'the atlas-eater with a jaw for news') are clearly *there*, but there within the autonomous logic of what are already strange (not just discontinuous) narratives. When Eliot was asked what the line 'Lady, three white leopards sat under a juniper tree' meant, all he could do in reply was repeat the line. There, it is the abruptness of the reference, its discontinuity with what surrounds it, rather than any logical impossibility in itself, that prompts the difficulty. Thomas had to explain stranger images. His explanation of the phrase 'the country-handed grave' (p. 50) asked us to imagine a grave with a country for each hand.[31] With such materials, there is a sense in which a poem's 'meaning', in Thomas's case as well, has to flower from spaces. But they are not spaces caused by gaps in the narrative, and not just spaces in between quickly changing images. They are the spaces left by the narratives not having any equivalents in the realistic world. Narratives of this kind *can* only be read literally. And they don't have to be in a 'Jabberwocky' language honourably to demand it.

Despite differences, we feel that what such poems share in is still essentially the central enterprise of Modernism. Even though the Modernist–Symbolist ideal developed from the increased subjectivism of Romanticism, no Romantic poet had made poems live to such a degree in imaginatively autonomous worlds. Donald Davie quotes the example of Keats's 'Ode to Autumn'. If the 'meaning' of a Symbolist poem lies in the sensibility it reflects (the only thing we can logically say it is 'about'), why isn't 'Ode to Autumn' a Symbolist poem? After all, no poem more closely conflates irreducible landscape or event with inner feeling. But Keats's natural landscape is available-to the poem rather than created-by it.[32] In hanging on to a continuous narrative line, Thomas was less ambitious than, say, Eliot in the structural method by which poems could be cut off from the logic of the world, even though his materials, in themselves, came from much stranger territories. But even while he claimed that 'narrative is essential' he saw it as a means whereby the ordinary expectations of the reader could be accommodated while the poem worked, otherwise, in less obviously logical ways. And, however paradoxical, it is significant that the authority Thomas quoted for this strategic function of narrative could still be Eliot himself. 'Narrative, in its widest sense,' he said, 'satisfies what Eliot, talking of "meaning", calls "one habit of the reader". Let the narrative take that one logical habit of the reader along with its movement, and the essence of the poem will do its work on him.'[33]

But let us move on from the influence of Thomas's Welshness or of Modernism. His reference above to the 'essence' of a poem should remind us that poems are not just exercises in technique. They communicate, however indirectly, a particular vision of the world. Even in Thomas's case, separation of theme from technique has not been so impossible as to prevent critics from evaluating his concerns as well as his methods. On the one hand, there is the view that his concern with birth, sex and death is obsessive and limited; and on the other, that concern with such things is high seriousness, and that (to quote A. Alvarez) Thomas 'had something rather original to say'.[34] Perhaps more relevant than just the question of limited range is that of the specific vision expressed. It is clear that this vision does not amount to a philosophy, a political ideology, or a religion in any full or ordinary sense. Indeed, as we have seen, much in the poems concerns a resistance to abstracted formulations. And this is where one particular critical emphasis deserves mention.

J. Hillis Miller has argued that 'what exists for Thomas as soon as anything exists at all is a single continuous realm which is at once consciousness, body, cosmos, and the words which express all three at once'.[35] So many of Thomas's comments outside the poems support such a claim that it could indeed be central to the focus a reader should bring to the poems themselves. We saw, for example, his claim that 'When I experience anything I experience it as a thing and a word at the same time', and his belief that 'Every idea, intuitive or intellectual, can be imaged and translated in terms of the body'. He also talked of 'a preconceived symbolism derived . . . from the cosmic significance of the human anatomy'.[36] But two different things need to be distinguished here. There can be no doubt that Thomas *does* make the body and the physical world his major source of symbols. In this way they act like the sphere of the occult in Yeats: an area from which to draw images; an area whose sheer consistency gives those images symbolic force. But J. Hillis Miller's description above suggests something deeper than just the source of images that make the poems operable. It suggests a particular *vision*, in which the physical and the intangible ('consciousness') or the physical and the abstract ('words') merge and mix. Martin Dodsworth takes Hillis Miller's claim further, in terms of a specific analogy with Blake.[37] In both poets the vision is one in which body, mind and spirit are genuinely 'interchangeable'. In such a view, a spiritual response to the world does not come from an abstracted soul but from the body when viewed as something more than a mere collection of mechanistic senses, and from the mind when prevented from being mere reason.

Dodsworth's full argument should be followed in his specific essay, and tested against the poems he analyses. Of general relevance here, however, is Dodsworth's contention that it is this phenomenon, a particular 'concept of mind', that is at the heart of the obscurity of the early poems. Such a view denies that the main difficulty comes from techniques that are structural or strategic. Consider, for contrast, these other (still friendly) explanations of Thomas's obscurity: that he wanted to delay our grasp of the whole by heightening, 'step by step, the conflict between our superficial interpretations until at last we are driven into comprehension' (Elder Olson); that he wanted to 'sustain states of emotion in his reader by demanding attention and concentration . . . by constantly drawing his reader's mind back to obsessive concerns through verbal repetition and variation' (W. T. Moynihan); that his aim is that of 'distancing the intimate', of preventing highly sexual material from being experienced too directly (R. N. Maud).[38] There is bound to be some truth in all of these. And they are not the only explanations that these particular critics put forward. R. N. Maud, for example, draws attention to the consistently patterned way in which Thomas juxtaposes positive and negative images. This is obviously relevant to the irreducibility of the poems: we perceive the significance of creative-versus-destructive images without needing the poems themselves to moralize discursively upon it. The cases put forward by Hillis Miller and Dodsworth, however, draw attention to something much stranger in the poet's way of perceiving reality in the first place. It is not a world-view by which we might live our daily lives; but, then, neither was Blake's. Perhaps that is why Thomas has so often to embody it in the form of pre-natal life. What those particular poems celebrate is certainly a world of undifferentiated consciousness, not yet broken down into separate physical, spiritual or rational compartments. That process of separation Thomas sees as being caused by language (in 'From love's first fever to her plague', p. 18):

> I learnt the verbs of will, and had my secret;
> The code of night tapped on my tongue;
> What had been one was many sounding minded.

Making language express more than one category of experience at a time would therefore be part of an attempt at *redeeming* language. So also would be the obsessive urge to make language *enact* rather than describe.

It is interesting, isn't it, that as soon as we start to speak of Thomas's themes or world-view they bring us back to language, as happens so often in the poems themselves. But we should not ignore the implications of such a world-view for the choice of themes, considered to some degree independently. We have noted that some such holistic vision would make natural the choice of pre-natal themes. Equally natural to such a view would be themes which conflate the geography of the human body with the processes of the universe. Similarly, Thomas's response to actual deaths, in which he envisions the dead person returning into the organic cycle. In turn, death itself is seen as a strange new burgeoning, in which all the senses become one, and with a spiritual refinement that can be imagined also for the five senses in actual life:

> My one and noble heart has witnesses
> In all love's countries, that will grope awake;
> And when blind sleep drops on the spying senses,
> The heart is sensual, though five eyes break.

('When all my five and country senses see', p. 74)

It is this refusal to accord bodily experience a merely physical status, or to reduce imaginative consciousness to cold reason, that is essentially Blakean. In this way, the technical freedom that the atmosphere of poetic Modernism had made possible served something deeper and older in Thomas's view of reality, though Modernism's delight in short-circuiting compartments of experience was also in itself relevant. When Thomas later lightened the pressures that this vision of reality placed on language itself, mainly by coming out into a more recognizable and objective world, he still remained with the themes that this vision had dictated. Thus the celebration of elemental oneness – of the natural, unthinking cohesion of physical and spiritual states – is the aim of 'Fern Hill' and 'Poem in October' as much as of the early pre-natal poems. But Dodsworth argues that when the later poems turn to individual human subjects, as opposed to 'the mysterious world of spirit' underlying all physical reality, or when they turn to an apparently more orthodox Christian frame of reference, they lose a sense of mystery and the ability to accommodate contradictions. Whether this is true – or whether it is indeed a particular world-view that produces those qualities in the first place – is something each reader has to decide.

It is at least significant that many other critics, among them William Empson,[39] have argued that the most valuable poems are the densely-textured early ones. This view seems particularly appropriate to the author of *Seven Types of Ambiguity*. But textural resistance should not automatically be taken for good value. Nor taken for granted as belonging only to the earlier work: the most detailed examination of 'Fern Hill', by Alastair Fowler,[40] reveals richnesses of texture and organization that will surprise even a reader long familiar with that poem. Thomas himself certainly felt pleased to have been delivering 'more meaning at first reading'. But, as Fowler puts it, this does not necessarily mean 'that his later poems had less at a second'. Exactly what the furthest sources of meaning in a poem may be also raises the question of allusion. Fowler finds 'Fern Hill' remarkably allusive, though mainly in terms of well-absorbed influences from other poems in the long tradition in which it stands. It is an allusiveness of a very different kind that is claimed by two detailed studies of the earlier 'Altarwise' sonnets. Elder Olson claims for those sonnets major levels of symbolism based on Greek myths of the sun-hero Hercules and on the relationship of the constellation Hercules to other constellations and astronomical phenomena.[41] H. H. Kleinman presupposes equally detailed esoteric knowledge on Thomas's part in the areas of Egyptian myths and funerary customs and marine biology.[42] Is it likely that, with his background, Thomas would have had this knowledge? Abstract conjecture on that score, however, is not as important as testing Olson or Kleinman's claims against the kind of knowledge the poems themselves seem to demand. Certainly to be guarded against is a danger increased by the sophistication of literary criticism over the last fifty years: the danger of finding impressive or sincere or profound only the most difficult texts.

One thing at least seems clear. Assessment of Thomas's achievement (pro or con, early or late) will always be concerned, essentially, with the way in which he uses language. That is not just a statement of the obvious. There is a sense, isn't there, in which what draws us back to a poet has more to do in the first place with the general attractions of his poetic voice – its sounds and movement – than with themes or attitudes or interesting difficulties. If we find these musical attractions there in Thomas, we can also be assured that he strenuously sought to guarantee them, that he believed passionately in a certain *kind* of poetry, the kind that delights in the solidity and memorability of language. For all his quarrels with language, there is an unembarrassed musical gusto in his use of it. It is presumably on that general stylistic impression that critical opinion first divides; from there on, on questions of meaning or difficulty, there is bound to be an element of rationalization to support either liking or disliking the *kind* of style involved. Perhaps part of Thomas's significance lies in his so completely challenging that taste in style.

The creation of new styles in poetry has always had much to do with a poet's readiness to disappoint his generation's general view of what is 'poetic'. And this was certainly true of Modernist poetry in this century. But there was always in Thomas something that respected the 'poetic' effect of the whole. He took full advantage of techniques of indirection that he knew would raise the charge of downright obscurity, and the visceral emphasis of much of the early poetry could also at some stage have been considered anti-poetic. But through the musical and celebratory tone of the whole, everything is levelled upwards. In a vague stylistic sense, as well as in some historically accurate thematic senses, he strikes us as a 'Romantic' poet. To some degree, later critics' attitude towards that 'Romantic' impression is affected by the originality or otherwise of Thomas's subject-matter. John Fuller, for example, finds the strange earlier poetry convincing and challenging, but finds 'Fern Hill' emotionally 'dishonest'.[43] Presumably, 'honesty' is invoked because the style strikes the critic as glamorously out of proportion to (and capable of falsifying) the traditional theme of recollected childhood. Whether it is so, of course, is a matter of opinion; and, more significantly, a matter of taste. But before we pursue this question of taste further, it is worth remarking how decisively Thomas's later poems did in the end retreat from the techniques of Modernism. In those later poems, techniques of indirection were replaced by a direct descriptive style, which conveys also a strong sense of the poet's own confessional presence. And the early imagined worlds, created by private

associations out of often disparate materials, were replaced by the
strong continuity of a realistic landscape. This may be relevant to
the critical reaction against Thomas's general style that set in after
his death. His stylistic legacy, unnaturally glamourized by his life-
style and early death in 1953, would have been associated mainly
with the later pastoral poems and *Under Milk Wood*. So the possible
irrelevance of Thomas's way with words to the different needs and
preoccupations of the new poets of the 1950s would also have been
associated with subjects equally uncongenial. Those younger poets
were urban or suburban, in theme and attitude as well as upbringing.
Part of their reaction against Thomas also involved reinstating in
poetry a wider range of themes having to do with ordinary personal
experiences. Their tendency was to level downwards. In that
particular connection, they were reacting against the large
mythopoeic vision of Yeats, Pound, and Eliot as much as against
the large 'bardic' persona of Dylan Thomas. Some of them had
started publishing in the 1940s and retained a serious respect for
Thomas's talents. (Philip Larkin, for example, praised Thomas for
his ability to 'speak out loud and clear' in the 1940s.)[44] But there
is no doubt that, in terms of style, the new poets of the 1950s took
a good deal of their incentive from a corrective reaction against the
Welshman's legacy, and from an urge to write less loudly.

Much in that reaction involved a reappraisal of what role a poet
plays in relationship to society. And nothing expresses or elucidates
a poet's perception of that role more than his dealings with language.
This lay at the heart of Donald Davie's resistance to Dylan Thomas.
We have seen (above, p. 103) Davie's direct attack on Thomas on the
matter of syntax in *Articulate Energy* (1955). But an earlier book
by Davie is also relevant: *Purity of Diction in English Verse* (1952),
though it does not itself deal with Thomas, elucidates linguistic and
stylistic qualities that are the exact reverse of Thomas's way with
words. Its essential challenge was to the notion that the concrete
image (as validated by Symbolism and Imagism) is the only central
power in poetry. Davie highlights a different, neglected strain in
English poetry of the last four centuries: one whose diction has the
more austere, often abstract, virtues of prose. Such poetry is moral
in its very avoidance of extreme individualism. One can see why this
should have led on to Davie's later examination of syntax – the
feature that has to carry the energy of a poem when the emphasis
has been taken off density of image. All this provides an opposed
frame of reference within which to judge the different linguistic effects
we associate with Thomas. That the relevance to Thomas of *Purity
of Diction in English Verse* was not accidental is shown by the later

'Postscript' that Davie added to a reprint of the study in 1966. There he rightly says that the book could well have been regarded as the unofficial poetic manifesto of the new poets who came into prominence in the 1950s. Davie connects his view that 'poetic effects' are 'moral' considerations with 'an angry reaction from the tawdry amoralism of a London Bohemia which had destroyed Dylan Thomas, the greatest talent of the generation before ours' (p. 198). To some degree, our view of Thomas's work is bound to be affected by being a view from this side of the very different poems produced by that reaction. Not just in the sense of a change in fashion: more important are some of the wider questions raised by Davie's position. (Many of them are raised in Davie's chapter on 'Hopkins as a Decadent Critic', which can be read with Thomas very much in mind.) To what degree is a poet justified in imposing his own will on language? Isn't part of his responsibility, rather, the purification of the language in such ways as also to make other poems by other poets possible? It seems clear that Thomas's style would be a disastrous example to follow – except, presumably, on the basis of our having equivalent talents and similar preoccupations. And in Thomas's own case, can one completely separate the outrageous Bohemian life-style from the wilfulness of the poems' techniques? Aren't these in fact interrelated – reflecting a moral, rather than just a literary, denial of central norms? This wider critical perspective is certainly important, though it does run the risk of pleading the virtues of standardization. After all, another poet–critic of the same generation as Davie – John Wain – has argued that Thomas's way with language, and his themes, can in any case be understood only in terms of his Welshness and the *regional* milieu in which he wrote.[45] It does at least seem significant that Davie, while welcoming the stylistic tendencies that distinguish British and American writing in the same language, does so by 'leaving aside the troublesome actualities or probabilities of Anglo-Welsh, Anglo-Scottish, New Zealand literature, Trinidadian and so on' (p. 201).

Davie's essentially moral view of style is relevant to the form that poetic reaction against Thomas took. Those particular poets of the 1950s who came to be known as the 'Movement' poets sought to reflect the different qualities of urbanity and poise, in which the strategies of irony and understatement replaced celebration and rhetorical colour. One can see why, for some of them, such a poet as Thomas Hardy could become an influence; or why, for others, a sense of stylistic continuity with the 1930s and 1940s should come through W. H. Auden rather than Dylan Thomas. Of course, without the major talents of a Philip Larkin, the lowering of poetry's rhetorical aims can lead to the nondescript as well as to the restrained. G. S. Fraser, in an essay that praises Thomas, reflects on the dangers of the otherwise healthy reaction against his style by borrowing Roy Campbell's famous epigram 'On Some South African Novelists':[46]

> You praise the firm restraint with which they write –
> I'm with you there, of course:
> They use the snaffle and the curb all right,
> But where's the bloody horse?

Introducing a still later generation of poets, A. Alvarez said very much the same thing about the 'Movement' poets, and praised Ted Hughes for his contrast with the 'gentility' of much of their verse. This was also where Alvarez harked back to Thomas as someone who 'had something rather original to say'.[47] But in the end Thomas's heightened style is not to be defended or queried only in the light of a later reaction against it. We have presumably to ask to what degree that style was made appropriate by the natural scale and energy of his chosen materials.

What was clearly aimed for in the style was memorability. In this, what we might call its insistent 'musical' properties cannot be divorced from the insistence also on strong wording. This is the ground on which, in the 1930s, he attacked the poetry of contemporaries like Stephen Spender and John Lehmann – even (with passionate honesty) that of his closest friend, Vernon Watkins – and in language that strangely foreshadows the above reservations concerning the 'Movement' poets of the 1950s: 'I can see the sensitive picking of words, but none of the strong, inevitable pulling that makes a poem an event, a happening, an action perhaps, not a still-life or an experience *put down*, placed, regulated'.[48] In this way, Thomas's style was itself, in its own time, a reaction. His attitude to the older Yeats and Eliot was different. It resembled that of Keats to Wordsworth and Coleridge: a profound respect, which however did not do without some mistrust of their intellectual confidence. (He thought Yeats the greatest poet of the century – though Hardy was his favourite – but thought some of Yeats's ideas mad.[49] And his admiration for Eliot did not prevent him from calling him 'Pope Eliot'.)[50] The same kind of corrective also coloured his view of his actual contemporary, W. H. Auden. In a special tribute for *New Verse*, he described Auden as 'a wide and deep poet', but naughtily added in a letter accompanying the tribute – 'Good luck to Auden on his seventieth birthday' (in 1937, when Auden was only 30!).[51] The point is that such correctives have to do with the danger of philosophical or ideological over-confidence, not with the authentic strength with which these three poets treated language. But perhaps more than any poet of his time, Thomas sought to find that strength in the weight and texture (rather than just the 'meaning') of each individual word. In this connection, it is odd that the critical formula describing his own methods most often emphasized by Thomas is the one least quoted. In reviews and letters he returned again and again to the need for poets to work 'out of' words, not 'towards them'.[52] Gabriel Pearson independently comes up with something like the same formulation in comparing Thomas and Auden. It is a good point on which to end because it brings together two young poets who, in the wake of Modernism, forged different voices in the early 1930s:[53]

> they begin to seem like part of one whole when viewed together in their beginnings. Each over-develops what the other neglects: crudely, thought as against feeling. Auden handles language from outside, like a craftsman or sportsman, while Thomas burrows into the body of the language itself from which he delivers oracles from the heat of its decomposition. They were together, it seems to me, the sundered halves of the great modernist poet that English poetry, after Eliot, failed to throw up.

Because Auden's stature would be difficult to minimize, it should not go against the policy of an 'Open' *Guide* to quote Pearson's further comment on the comparison: 'Of the two, I believe, against the grain of current prejudice, Thomas denied less of himself than Auden and emerges from a reading of his poetry and prose as the richer, more humanly grounded artist'. In any case, a further quotation from the same source is an accurate description of the still 'open' state of Thomas's reputation. And its last four words are as wise a guidance as any:

> The legend is still an un-negotiated legacy, fraught with predictable discomfort however you play it, whether with aloofness, or bold enthusiasm. Either way, Thomas remains powerful, disreputable and not to be patronized.

Notes

The following abbreviations are used:

Collected Letters – Paul Ferris (ed.), *The Collected Letters of Dylan Thomas* (1985)

Early Prose Writings – Walford Davies (ed.), *Dylan Thomas: Early Prose Writings* (1971)

New Critical Essays – Walford Davies (ed.) *Dylan Thomas: New Critical Essays* (1972)

Poet in the Making – R. N. Maud (ed.), *Poet in the Making: The Notebooks of Dylan Thomas* (1968)

Twentieth Century Views – C. B. Cox (ed.), *Dylan Thomas*, 'Twentieth Century Views' Series (1966).

Chapter 1: Biographical and Introductory (Pages 1–11)

1   Dylan Thomas, letter to Daniel Jones: *Collected Letters*, p. 197.
2   See *Early Prose Writings*, pp. 97–121.
3   Published as *Dylan Thomas: 'Dog Among the Fairies'* in 1949.
4   Quoted in Paul Ferris, *Dylan Thomas* (1977) p. 176.
5   In *The Use of Poetry and the Use of Criticism* (1933). See J. Hayward (ed.), *T. S. Eliot: Selected Prose* (1953) p. 93.
6   Collected in Daniel Jones (ed.), *A Prospect of the Sea* (1955).
7   Quoted in Paul Ferris, *Dylan Thomas* (1977) p. 292.

Chapter 2: Poems on Poetry (Pages 11–25)

1   W. B. Yeats, *Collected Poems*, (1950 edn) p. 142.
2   James Joyce, *Portrait of the Artist as a Young Man*, ch. 4.
3   See 'Poetic Manifesto', *Early Prose Writings*, pp. 154–55.
4   W. B. Yeats, *Collected Poems* (1950 edn) p. 392.
5   The phrase is in Keats's 'Bright star!' sonnet.
6   Letter to Vernon Watkins: *Collected Letters*, p. 264.
7   Letter to Henry Treece: *Collected Letters*, p. 298.
8   'Answers to An Enquiry', *New Verse* (October 1934) pp. 8–9. Reprinted in *Early Prose Writings*, pp. 149–50.
9   Letter to Henry Treece: *Collected Letters*, p. 281.

10 See *Poet in the Making*, p. 347.
11 Quoted by Alastair Reid. See E. W. Tedlock (ed.), *Dylan Thomas: The Legend and the Poet* (1960) p. 54.
12 'Lines Composed a Few Miles Above Tintern Abbey' (ll. 105–7).
13 'On Poetry' (a broadcast script), in Aneirin Talfan Davies (ed.), *Quite Early One Morning* (1954) p. 169.

Chapter 3: The Early Poetry (Pages 26–47)

1 *T. S. Eliot: Selected Prose* (1953) p. 93.
2 *Twentieth Century Views*, pp. 85, 86.
3 *Poet in the Making*, p. 250.
4 *A Prospect of the Sea* (1955) p. 85.
5 Thomas, in a letter to Richard Church, defending himself against the charge of automatic writing. See *Collected Letters*, p. 205.
6 Letter to Pamela Hansford Johnson: *Collected Letters*, p. 108.
7 In the poem's first published form, in *New Verse* (June 1934) pp. 6–8. This would also be a good example to track back to its very different earliest form in the Notebooks. See *Poet in the Making*, pp. 255–57. One small point of interest is that 'damned' in the third line (Notebook and final versions) became 'dammed' in the *New Verse* and *18 Poems* version.
8 In *The Use of Poetry and the Use of Criticism* (1933). See J. Hayward (ed.), *T. S. Eliot: Selected Prose* (1953) p. 94.
9 C. Day Lewis, *Collected Poems* (1954), p. 171.
10 Charles Dickens, *Dombey and Son*, ch. 1.
11 John Donne, 'Second Anniversarie'.
12 John Donne, 'A Funerall Elegie'.
13 A selection of his best reviews appear in *Early Prose Writings*.
14 Letter to Pamela Hansford Johnson: *Collected Letters*, p. 39.

Chapter 4: Comparisons: Some Earlier and Later Poems (Pages 48–62)

1 The poem can be conveniently found in *Selected Poems by Thom Gunn and Ted Hughes* (1962), p. 35.
2 Thomas describes it in a letter to Pamela Hansford Johnson: *Collected Letters*, p. 62.
3 See letter to Vernon Watkins: *Collected Letters*, p. 518. That the description 'a Laugharne poem: the first place poem I've written' refers to 'Poem in October' is made clear by Thomas's including this poem in his next letter, four days later (p. 519).
4 Letter to Vernon Watkins: *Collected Letters*, p. 519.
5 Letter to Henry Treece: *Collected Letters*, p. 301.
6 John Wain, *Twentieth Century Views*, pp. 10–11.
7 David Aivaz, 'The Poetry of Dylan Thomas', reprinted in E. W. Tedlock (ed.), *Dylan Thomas: The Legend and the Poet* (1960) pp. 198–99.
8 Clark Emery, *The World of Dylan Thomas* (1971) p. 200.

Chapter 5: Thomas and Friends (Pages 62–76)

1 For the earlier (1933) poem, see *Poet in the Making*, p. 168.
2 For the earlier (1933) poem, see *Poet in the Making*, p. 204.

3   Letter to Vernon Watkins: *Collected Letters*, p. 327.
4   *Ibid.*, p. 328.
5   W. B. Yeats, *Collected Poems* (1950 edn) p. 338.
6   *Ibid.*, p. 236.
7   *Romeo and Juliet*, III, i, 98.
8   John Donne, 'The Triple Fool'.
9   See *Poet in the Making*, p. 155.

Chapter 6: 'Fern Hill' and Later Poems (Pages 77–93)

1   'Three Poems', in Aneirin Talfan Davies (ed.), *Quite Early One Morning* (1954) pp. 156–57. A version of the title poem 'In Country Heaven' is printed in Daniel Jones (ed.), *Dylan Thomas: The Poems* (1971).
2   Letter to his publishers, Dent: *Collected Letters*, p. 569.
3   'Three Poems', *Quite Early One Morning*, p. 157.
4   See Douglas Cleverdon, *The Growth of Milk Wood* (1969) p. 5.
5   John Wain, 'Druid of Her Broken Body', in *New Critical Essays*, pp. 19–20.
6   *Twentieth Century Views*, p. 87.
7   J. M. Brinnin, *Dylan Thomas in America* (1955), p. 128.
8   *Twentieth Century Views*, p. 88.
9   David Holbrook's psycho-analytical approach to Thomas has been developed in two books: *Llareggub Revisited: Dylan Thomas and the State of Modern Poetry* (1962) and *Dylan Thomas and the Code of Night* (1972).
10 Cf. 'a mankind witch' (*The Winter's Tale* II, iii, 68) and 'are you mankind?' (asked of a female – *Coriolanus* IV, ii, 16).
11 Gordon S. Haight (ed.), *The George Eliot Letters*, vol. v (1956) p. 107.
12 K. W. Gransden, 'An Interview' (poem), in Philip Larkin (ed.), *The Oxford Book of Twentieth-Century English Verse* (1973) p. 553–54.

Chapter 7: Contexts and Conclusions (Pages 94–123)

1   Letter to Daniel Jones: *Collected Letters*, p. 197.
2   In the story 'Where Tawe Flows', in *Portrait of the Artist as a Young Dog*.
3   Letter to Vernon Watkins: *Collected Letters*, p. 222.
4   Caitlin Thomas, *Not Quite Posthumous Letters to My Daughter* (1963) p. 27.
5   Caitlin Thomas, *Leftover Life to Kill* (1957) p. 35.
6   John Malcolm Brinnin's phrase. Quoted in Paul Ferris, *Dylan Thomas* (1977) p. 232.
7   Letter to Hamish Miles: *Collected Letters*, p. 117.
8   Reported by Aneirin Talfan Davies. Quoted in Paul Ferris, *Dylan Thomas* (1977) p. 119.
9   Most notably the author Glyn Jones and Aneirin Talfan Davies, the Welsh BBC producer who commissioned many of Thomas's broadcasts. But from the very start, Thomas's father would have been as good a source as any for this kind of information.
10 The first printing of the sonnet sequence in *Life and Letters Today* (December 1935) pp. 73–75 had 'Love's a reflection of the mushroom features'.

11   F. W. Bateson, *English Poetry: A Critical Introduction* (2nd edn 1966) p. 67.
12   Alastair Reid, in E. W. Tedlock (ed.), *Dylan Thomas: The Legend and the Poet* (1960) p. 53.
13   Letter to Margaret Taylor: *Collected Letters*, p. 735.
14   First noticed by David Holbrook. See his essay 'The Code of Night' in *New Critical Essays*, pp. 182–89.
15   Letter to Vernon Watkins: *Collected Letters*, p. 223.
16   'Chains and the Poet', in *New Critical Essays*, p. 65.
17   Donald Davie, *Articulate Energy: An Inquiry into the Syntax of English Poetry* (1976 edn) pp. 125–26.
18   In a review of Davie's book in *Essays in Criticism* (January 1958) p. 83.
19   Letter to Henry Treece: *Collected Letters*, p. 281.
20   Reprinted in *Early Prose Writings*, pp. 83–6.
21   Letter to Henry Treece: *Collected Letters*, p. 297.
22   In 'A Retrospect'. Reprinted in T. S. Eliot (ed.), *Literary Essays of Ezra Pound* (1954) pp. 3–14.
23   *Ibid.*
24   See, for example, his review of Sydney Salt's *Thirty Pieces*. Reprinted in *Early Prose Writings*, p. 167.
25   Letter to Vernon Watkins: *Collected Letters*, p. 487.
26   'The Symbolism of Poetry', *Essays and Introductions* (1961) p. 163.
27   'The Orchards', Daniel Jones (ed.), *A Prospect of the Sea* (1955) p. 85.
28   Quoted in Henry Treece, *Dylan Thomas* (1949), p. 23. This chapter in Treece's book is on Thomas's 'Relations to Surrealism'. For a detailed discussion of Thomas and Surrealism, see M. Gee, *The Influence of Surrealism on English Writing of the 'Thirties and 'Forties*, unpublished B. Litt. thesis, University of Oxford, 1974 (Bodleian Library). Both Treece and Gee stress the conscious craftsmanship of Thomas's writing, the element that marks him off from the Surrealists. For Thomas's own hostile view of Surrealist writing, see *Collected Letters*, pp. 204–5 and *Early Prose Writings*, pp. 159–60.
29   In Graham Martin (ed.), *Eliot in Perspective* (1970) pp. 74–9.
30   Letter to Glyn Jones: *Collected Letters*, p. 97.
31   Letter to Henry Treece: *Collected Letters*, pp. 300–1.
32   In Graham Martin (ed.), *Eliot in Perspective* (1970) p. 80.
33   'Answers to an Enquiry', reprinted in *Early Prose Writings*, p. 149.
34   Introduction to *The New Poetry* (revised edn 1966) p. 23.
35   J. Hillis Miller, *Poets of Reality: Six Twentieth-century Writers* (1966) pp. 190–91.
36   Letter to Glyn Jones: *Collected Letters*, p. 98.
37   M. Dodsworth, 'The Concept of Mind in the Poetry of Dylan Thomas', *New Critical Essays*, pp. 107–35.
38   Details of the books by these three critics are given in the 'Suggestions for Further Reading' at the end of this *Guide*.
39   *Twentieth Century Views*, p. 85.
40   *New Critical Essays*, pp. 228–61.
41   Elder Olson, *The Poetry of Dylan Thomas* (1954).
42   H. H. Kleinman, *The Religious Sonnets of Dylan Thomas* (1963).
43   *New Critical Essays*, p. 220.

44   Introduction to *The North Ship* (1966 edn) p. 8.
45   'Druid of Her Broken Body', *New Critical Essays*, pp. 1–20.
46   'English Poetry 1930–1960' in B. Bergonzi (ed.), *The Twentieth Century* ('Sphere' History of Literature in the English Language, 1970), p. 304.
47   Introduction to *The New Poetry* (revised edn 1966) p. 23.
48   Letter to Vernon Watkins: *Collected Letters*, p. 278.
49   *Early Prose Writings*, p. 152.
50   Letter to Vernon Watkins: *Collected Letters*, p. 222.
51   Letter to Geoffrey Grigson: *Collected Letters*, p. 259.
52   See, for example, the selection of Thomas's reviews of poetry in *Early Prose Writings*, pp. 165ff.
53   *The Spectator*, 20 November 1971, pp. 731–32.

Suggestions for Further Reading

(Except where otherwise indicated, the publishers are Dent)

The first stages of a close study of the work will gain in being followed by an overview of the life and career. The standard biographies are *The Life of Dylan Thomas* by Constantine FitzGibbon (1965) and *Dylan Thomas* by Paul Ferris (Hodder and Stoughton, 1977). But Thomas's is also the perfect case in which to remember Yeats's dictum, that 'the poet who writes the poem is never the bundle of accident and incoherence that sits down to breakfast'. Perhaps the main phenomenon that he represents is the strange contrast between the careless, untidy life and the careful, almost care-worn craft he invested in the work. A balance between these two aspects is made possible by a reading of his letters. His *Letters to Vernon Watkins* (Faber/Dent, 1957) is particularly interesting for detailed comments on the poems. FitzGibbon's edition of the *Selected Letters* (1966) has been superseded by Paul Ferris's *The Collected Letters* (1985). Those to Pamela Hansford Johnson are probably the best introduction to the personality of the young man.

The most important volume for a further study of the poems themselves, however, is R. N. Maud's *Poet in the Making* (1968) – an edition of Thomas's four poetry 'Notebooks' covering the period 1930–1934. Of special interest here are the early manuscript versions of a great number of the poems that now comprise the final *Collected Poems 1934–1952*. Comparison with the final versions often illuminates poetic method and meaning. Also revealing is the choice Thomas made as to which poems to preserve and develop.

You should certainly not ignore the prose. Apart from its own intrinsic rewards (often claimed to have been undervalued) its different, comic vision supplements the more sombre vision of the poetry. The prose often also parallels the stylistic development of the poetry. The volumes recommended here therefore are listed in the broad chronological order of the prose works they contain. The early short stories are included mainly in *A Prospect of the Sea* (ed. Daniel Jones, 1955) but others will be found in *Dylan Thomas: Early Prose Writings* (ed. Walford Davies, 1971). The change in theme and style that we saw Thomas's poetry to be concerned with around 1938 is reflected, in the prose, in the autobiographical short stories of *Portrait of the Artist as a Young Dog* (1940). The autobiographical material extended naturally into the unfinished 'novel' *Adventures in the Skin Trade* (1955). Good examples of the filmscripts Thomas was writing around 1944 would be *Twenty Years A-Growing* (1964) and *The Doctor and the Devils* (1953). The best of the radio broadcasts from the mid-1940s to the early 1950s were collected in *Quite Early One Morning* (ed. Aneirin Talfan Davies, 1954). Something worth exploring are the techniques of presentation reflected in the filmscripts and some of the broadcasts as they would have influenced Thomas's radio 'play for voices' *Under Milk Wood* (1954).

Of the numerous critical studies, one offering a general survey approach might be selected first. Henry Treece's *Dylan Thomas: 'Dog Among the Fairies'* (1949; rev. edn Ernest Benn 1956) has the interest of being the earliest attempt to evaluate the full achievement. John Ackerman's *Dylan Thomas: His Life and Work* (Oxford University Press, 1964) develops particularly the Welsh background, and his later *Welsh Dylan* (John Jones, 1979) emphasizes the importance of the sense of 'place' and the achievement of the later work as that of a lyric poet 'passionately learning to grow old'.

The best book to read next (and one of the best books) would be R. N. Maud's *Entrances to Dylan Thomas' Poetry* (Scorpion Press, 1963). Scholarly and helpful in its approach to problems of detail and technique, it also contains a valuable 'Chronology of Composition' as Appendix I. William T. Moynihan's *The Craft and Art of Dylan Thomas* (Oxford University Press, 1966) is a sensitive discussion of the poet's auditory, rhetorical, and metaphorical techniques. Elder Olson's *The Poetry of Dylan Thomas* (University of Chicago Press, 1954) characterizes lucidly and persuasively the broad features of the poetry. More open to question, however, is the validity of the mythical and astronomical images that Olson claims to be one of the levels of structure in the 'Altarwise' sonnets. Two outstanding analysts of Thomas's use of language are: John Bayley in *The Romantic Survival* (Constable and Oxford University Press, 1957); and Winifred Nowottny in *The Language Poets Use* (Athlone Press, 1962). The 'Twentieth Century Views' volume on

Thomas, ed. C. B. Cox (Prentice-Hall, 1966) is a balanced selection from some of the most interesting criticism. A wide variety of critical approaches and assessments is reflected in *Dylan Thomas: New Critical Essays*, ed. Walford Davies (1972). The most rewarding way to consider a view of poetry that would be hostile to Thomas's achievement is to read Donald Davie's *Purity of Diction in English Verse* (1952; reprinted with a postscript, Routledge 1967) and *Articulate Energy* (Routledge 1955; reprinted with a postscript 1976). Though only briefly or by implication concerned with Thomas, they argue the theoretic grounds of something more useful than merely arbitrary dislike.

In tackling the most immediate difficulties of individual poems, the reader will find useful the poem-by-poem format of W. Y. Tindall's *A Reader's Guide to Dylan Thomas* (Thames and Hudson, 1962) and Clark Emery's *The World of Dylan Thomas* (University of Miami Press 1962, Dent 1971).

R. N. Maud's *Dylan Thomas in Print* (1972) is a full bibliography of Thomas's work. It also lists, for the period 1934–1971, everything written about him 'that seemed to be of possible interest to the literary historian or the curious general reader'.

Index